Rethinking Basic Design in Architectural Education

Rethinking Basic Design in Architectural Education provides historical and computational insights into beginning design education for architecture. Inviting the readers to briefly forget what is commonly known as basic design, it delivers the account of two educators, Denman W. Ross and Arthur W. Dow, from the turn of the twentieth century in Northeast America, interpreting key aspects of their methodology for teaching foundations for design and art. This alternate intellectual context for the origins of basic design as a precursor to computational design complements the more haptic, more customized, and more open-source design and fabrication technologies today.

Basic design described and illustrated here as a form of low-tech computation offers a setting for the beginning designer to consciously experience what it means to design. Individualized dealings with materials, tools, and analytical techniques foster skills and attitudes relevant to creative and technologically adept designers. The book is a timely contribution to the theory and methods of beginning design education when fast-changing design and production technology demands change in architecture schools' foundations curricula.

Mine Özkar is Professor of Architecture at Istanbul Technical University, Turkey. Collaborating with design professionals, computer scientists, and art historians, her research focuses on visual, spatial, and material aspects of design computation, and their integration to foundational design education. She holds a PhD in design and computation from Massachusetts Institute of Technology (MIT), USA.

Routledge Research in Architecture

The *Routledge Research in Architecture* series provides the reader with the latest scholarship in the field of architecture. The series publishes research from across the globe and covers areas as diverse as architectural history and theory, technology, digital architecture, structures, materials, details, design, monographs of architects, interior design and much more. By making these studies available to the worldwide academic community, the series aims to promote quality architectural research.

Cut and Paste Urban Landscape
The Work of Gordon Cullen
Mira Engler

Wooden Church Architecture of the Russian North
Regional Schools and Traditions
(14th – 19th centuries)
Evgeny Khodakovsky

Mid-Century Modernism in Turkey
Architecture Across Cultures in the 1950s and 1960s
Meltem Ö. Gürel

Bruno Taut's Design Inspiration for the Glashaus
David Nielsen

Conflicted Identities
Housing and the Politics of Cultural Representation
Alexandra Staub

Through the Healing Glass
Shaping the Modern Body through Glass Architecture, 1925–35
John Stanislav Sadar

Architecture as Cultural and Political Discourse
Case studies of conceptual norms and aesthetic practices
Daniel Grinceri

Sacred Architecture in a Secular Age
Anamnesis of Durham Cathedral
Marie Clausén

The Architecture of San Juan de Puerto Rico
Five centuries of urban and architectural experimentation
Arleen Pabón

Perspectives on Research Assessment in the Arts, Music and Architecture
Discussing Doctorateness
Fredrik Nilsson, Halina Dunin-Woyseth and Nel Janssens

Rethinking Basic Design in Architectural Education
Foundations Past and Future
Mine Özkar

Rethinking Basic Design in Architectural Education
Foundations Past and Future

Mine Özkar

NEW YORK AND LONDON

First published 2017
by Routledge
711 Third Avenue, New York, NY 10017

and by Routledge
2 Park Square, Milton Park, Abingdon, Oxon OX14 4RN

Routledge is an imprint of the Taylor & Francis Group, an informa business

© 2017 Mine Özkar

The right of Mine Özkar to be identified as author of this work has been asserted by her in accordance with sections 77 and 78 of the Copyright, Designs and Patents Act 1988.

All rights reserved. No part of this book may be reprinted or reproduced or utilised in any form or by any electronic, mechanical, or other means, now known or hereafter invented, including photocopying and recording, or in any information storage or retrieval system, without permission in writing from the publishers.

Trademark notice: Product or corporate names may be trademarks or registered trademarks, and are used only for identification and explanation without intent to infringe.

British Library Cataloguing in Publication Data
A catalogue record for this book is available from the British Library

Library of Congress Cataloging in Publication Data
Names: Ozkar, Mine, author.
Title: Rethinking basic design in architectural education : foundations past and future / Mine èOzkar.
Description: New York : Routledge, 2017. | Series: Routledge research in architecture | Includes bibliographical references.
Identifiers: LCCN 2016027205 | ISBN 9781138825420 (hardback : alk. paper) | ISBN 9781315740003 (ebook)
Subjects: LCSH: Architecture--Study and teaching. | Architecture--Curricula. | Design--Study and teaching.
Classification: LCC NA2005 .O96 2017 | DDC 720.71--dc23
LC record available at https://lccn.loc.gov/2016027205

ISBN: 978-1-138-82542-0 (hbk)
ISBN: 978-1-315-74000-3 (ebk)

Typeset in Sabon
by Taylor & Francis Books

Contents

List of Figures	vii
Acknowledgments	ix

Introduction	1

PART I
Early Beginnings — 9

1	Seeing Design in Art: Visions of Denman Waldo Ross	11
2	Abstract Forms and Form Relations: Arthur Wesley Dow	35
3	The Psychology for Basic Design in the Late Nineteenth Century	45

PART II
Looking to the Future — **81**

4	The Disillusioning Pasts of Basic Design	83
5	Computational Design Foundations	111
6	Conclusion: Pragmatics of a Foundational Studio	141

Index	154

Figures

1.1	The arrangement of prints of wallpaper designs and their compositional parts; spatial relations from wallpaper designs	16
1.2	Some elements of Pure Design	17
1.3	Details from Ross *et al.* (1900), Plates 1 and 2	18
1.4	Details from Ross *et al.* (1900), Plates 7, 8, and 9	19
1.5	Details from Ross *et al.* (1900), Plates 10, 6, 22, and 6	19
1.6	Detail from Ross (1907). The exercises go beyond combining given sets of shapes as students explore various relations between shapes at different levels	20
1.7	Detail from geometric sketches with shading, undated	21
1.8	Detail from geometric floral design, undated	22
1.9	Geometric analysis with triangle of √4 of figure from Sistine Chapel ceiling by Michelangelo, undated	24
1.10	Design analysis with triangle of √4 of figure from Sistine Chapel ceiling by Michelangelo, undated	26
1.11	"The Jetty of Calais" by J.M.W. Turner with diagonals of √4, rectangle of √2, 3 √4 rectangles approximately, undated; "Little Devil's Bridge" by J.M.W. Turner with chalk lines drawn with the triangle of √4, undated	29
1.12	Photograph of young man in profile with geometric analysis and inset of "Ritratto di Lionello d'Este" by Vittore Pisano, undated	31
1.13	Photograph of young man seated in 3/4 pose with geometric analysis drawn with the XM triangle, undated	32

viii *Figures*

2.1	Pixellated image of young man with photograph inset, undated	42
3.1	Details from Ross *et al.* (1900), Plates 10 and 12	49
3.2	Clipping of "Fragments of Leaves Partially Eaten by Insects...", undated	54
3.3	Photograph of woman seated in 3/4 pose with geometric analysis of triangles of a square and of XM, undated	67
3.4	Photograph of man with hat in profile with geometric analysis of rectangle √3 and drawn with the triangle of √3, undated	70
5.1	Various decompositions of a shaded circle	116
5.2	A visual rule and its application in design	134
5.3	Two visual rules and their application in similar designs	134
6.1	Two visual rules and their applications in similar designs	145
6.2	Two triangles out of one	149

Acknowledgments

This volume is mostly based on the dissertation I completed for my doctoral degree in Architecture: Design and Computation at Massachusetts Institute of Technology between 1999 and 2004. The historical focus on theories of education developed by Denman Waldo Ross and Arthur Wesley Dow and my perspective on the core of basic design education are preserved. Revisions to the original text include the redesign and reorganization of chapters, added clarifications and updated literature reviews. I also added a chapter reciting some of my more recent research with relevance to basic design. I would like to thank Springer and Kim Williams Brooks for the permissions.

I am indebted to the many people who supported me during my doctoral research and later on in the preparation of the book. First and foremost, I would like to thank my mentors George Stiny, Edith Ackermann, and Whitman Richards. The numerous conversations with each have been of the highest value to me. I am deeply saddened in losing both Edith and Whitman in 2016. I am also grateful to Lionel March, talking to whom benefited me in the earlier years of my studies, and to Türel Saranlı who has inspired and supported my passion for basic design education ever since he was my instructor in 1993. I thank Mark Goulthorpe for his enthusiasm and belief in the dissertation, a most valuable encouragement to me. Abby Smith at the Fogg Museum Archives, and Stephanie Gaskins at Ipswich Historical Society, MA, thoughtfully assisted my access to the original documents prior to 2004.

In the preparations for the book, I am obliged to Megan Schwenke, the archivist and records manager at Harvard Art Museums, who patiently and diligently assisted me in relocating the Ross documents

x *Acknowledgments*

and, along with Isabella Donadio, in getting the necessary permissions for the images. Special thanks to Wendy Fuller and Sade Lee at Routledge for supporting the book project, and to Christina O'Brien and Grace Harrison for their diligence in the final stretch.

It would have been impossible for me to pursue the dissertation without the Presidential Fellowship awarded to me for five years at MIT. Many thanks also go to my colleagues and friends there: Jacquelyn Martino, Lira Nikolovska, Axel Kilian and Joao Rocha as well as Ali Pırnar, Zeynep Çelik, Nyssim Lefford, and Erdem Erten, for thought-provoking and encouraging discussions across disciplines, Esra Özkan and Amy Özay, for enthusiastic editorial help. Erkin Özay has continued his editorial service in the book preparation process.

Immediately following my doctorate, I had the opportunity to work side by side with some of my basic design instructors at the Middle East Technical University. I am truly indebted to Tuğyan Aytaç Dural, Selahattin Önür, Erkan Gencol, Nihal Bursa, and all my students for an experience in those first years that gave me new perspectives on what I had been writing about.

I would also like to acknowledge Arzu Gönenç Sorguç and Şebnem Yalınay Çinici for encouraging my continued pursuit of the relation between computation and basic design, the Architectural Design Computing Program and the Department of Architecture at Istanbul Technical University where I presently work as I finalize the book project, and Onur Yüce Gün and Benay Gürsoy for countless deliberations on the nitty-gritty of basic design. Being able to share an interest at such a profound level elevates the meaning of it all, hopefully towards an ever-growing positive impact.

Introduction

Basic design is another name for foundations in architecture, product design, and seldom, planning education. It is sometimes short for basic principles of design, and is notoriously a part of a modernist take on design as composition. This book does not attempt to give a complete definition and a comprehensive historiography for what *one* basic design might have once been, or now is. Instead, it suggests that we all briefly forget what we know of basic design, or what we assume the name basic design means, and start over by deliberating on what may be the foundations to learning design in an era of ubiquitous information technologies. Therein, it reconstructs a unique historical, theoretical, and practical context for basic design and foundations in architectural education.

The act of designing has a centuries-old relationship with abstraction, on the one hand, and physical interaction, on the other. Today, architectural design research and practice continue to expand into both the mathematical world of computational modeling and the material world of digital fabrication and production. Whereas computation was mostly perceived in architecture a few decades ago as a technical gimmick that one can do without, it is now central to discussions on creative reasoning. Even if computationally generated or represented forms often appear to be purely graphic and lacking a material context, there is a growing interest in linking these forms to the material and subjective aspects of the physical world. As an integral part of a more conscious – and yes, still creative – design act, computation is now one of the key contemporary challenges in design pedagogy. It gradually seeps into all levels of architectural design curricula with increasing demand for integration

2 Introduction

of not only mathematical but also visual, material, and, kinesthetic aspects of design. The integration is manifold. This text focuses on the integration within the scope of what can be included in the very first year of higher education and proposes an updated basic design as its instrument.

When the incoming students at an institution of higher education for architecture are mostly high school graduates who so far have been occupied with an educational focus on STEM (Science, Technology, Engineering, Math) subjects, the first year of architectural education can be a bit of a culture shock. Although there are many different approaches practiced by the thousands of higher education institutes for architecture around the world, higher education institutes which have taken on the task of offering an educational program towards a degree in architecture rely on this STEM background but also introduce students to the profession through foundational courses on design and graphic communication skills that are often unprecedented in prior education. Basic design is one such form of instruction in the first year. A modernist program, as it came to be understood within architectural discourse, it is a common preliminary curriculum in art and architecture education. Commonly, through experimental use of abstract forms and materials to respond to abstract problems, a basic design course tries to equip the beginning student with fundamental design skills that will universally apply to any form and material in future contexts. There may be variations in execution, especially in the adherence to the abstract vocabulary.

The popular history of basic design education in architecture points to the Bauhaus in Weimar for its beginnings. Multiple accounts of the renowned school from the 1920s show that its pedagogy has changed greatly over time from its initial to its later years. Digressing from the earlier interest in the students' self-conscious creative thinking that was inspired by then progressive kindergarten teachings, the school eventually adopted a stricter modernist agenda to use the basics as grounds for the standardization of design in an ideally equalitarian society. It is impossible to talk about one Bauhaus and its one type of basic design practice. It is also inaccurate to limit basic design in architecture education as the pedagogical bequest of a unique Bauhaus legacy. As will be discussed in this book, from a contemporary viewpoint and with a

Introduction 3

refreshed historical epistemology, basic design methodology holds a great deal of potential. It can endorse individualized reasoning as an integral part of the emerging, computationally enhanced curriculum of the twenty-first century.

As a first step, in blurring the said historical context for basic design, it is key to identify another earlier tradition of basic design instruction in the educational practices of Denman Waldo Ross and Arthur Wesley Dow in North America. Ross taught in the Architecture and Fine Arts Departments of Harvard University between 1899 and 1935, whereas Dow taught composition, first, at Ipswich, MA, starting from before the turn of the century, and later in Teachers College at Columbia University in New York between 1908 and 1922. They were in the same circles and knew each other as early as 1896 when Dow visited Ross in Venice. They worked closely in Massachusetts after that, especially in 1901, as Dow observed Ross's class in Boston and they reportedly painted together. Having correlated design teaching ideas, they even collaborated on a published article on architectural education and "pure design" as a part of its curriculum (Ross and Dow, 1901, 38). Neither Ross nor Dow actually used the term "basic design" to refer to what they taught, but, as discussed in the forthcoming chapters, their respective terms of pure design and composition overlap with the framework drawn here for basic design. The significance of Ross and Dow is that they separately developed abstraction as a method of intellectual inquiry into design, and did so a little earlier and a little differently than their modernist counterparts in early twentieth-century Europe. Their teaching approach marks a turning point in the perception of art and design as visual reasoning. One can even consider this point in time as the emergence of an early version of design thinking as a discipline, prior to any encounters with computation. In terms of ideas, Ross and Dow are vanguards of a modernist design education. At the same time, having applied their reformist approach, mostly in conservative visual styles of applied arts from a past era, they are overshadowed in design history by the visually compelling and progressive work of the avant-gardes that came later and with much hype.

There were expected parallels between the method of abstraction that Ross and Dow (and their contemporaries, such as Ernest Fenollosa)

4 Introduction

were interested in developing in America, and the "reformative aesthetic" of abstraction in early twentieth-century Europe (Martin, 1980). However, Ross and Dow's formalisms were also quite locally shaped. For one thing, both Ross and Dow were involved in the American Arts and Crafts movement and the Orientalist movement and their artistic styles form a vocabulary that reflects that. At the same time, they belonged to an intellectual community unique to that geography at the time. This community included philosophers, psychologists, and scientists, such as William James, George Santayana, Hugo Münsterberg, and John Dewey, who are known to be critical of pure and inflexible intellectualism. These men shared an interest in individual reasoning processes and the positive role of sensory experience in learning. In addition, North America had had a progressive and visually oriented culture of education since the late eighteenth century. Already existing reformist tendencies in public education included the objective instruction of art and design and even a mention of "abstract design" recognized retrospectively in 1929 (Jaffee, 2005). Older than a century, some aspects of the methods that Ross and Dow proposed for design and art education are certainly dated today. Nevertheless, the context in which Ross and Dow's ideas grew can be related today with regards to the technological drive – a determination to govern the "how" – and to the paradigm of student-centered learning in higher education.

One of the motivations to write this book is to give a background for visual and spatial reasoning as the application of creativity in the field of design and computation. Creativity can be defined in many ways. When deemed as the ability to consciously develop unique strategies in changing contexts, it requires the involved conceptual structures to be temporary. Parts and relationships change and the descriptions of the world are flexible. One can temporarily set relations and descriptions when taking a particular action. Design education then is training in how to reason. It can focus on the individual learner just as much as on the knowledge and techniques of the profession so that uncertain ways and marginal thoughts, necessary in creative endeavors, are not compromised but nourished and given a good basis. Sensory experience is a crucial function of this training. This perspective on art and design education already resonated with the Pragmatist philosophy in the nineteenth century and reviving a pragmatist take on the senses is relevant when reconsidering reasoning in design and computation today. The end of the nineteenth century in the Western world represents an interlude between the formalisms of the past and the present in how design and its foundational concepts are perceived. Looking back to that period in history, particularly in Northeast America, is refreshing as a break from the usual references of architectural history and of design computation. This re-reading sets a frame for understanding some origins for current ideas, and also provides tracks for alternative paths.

A secondary motivation has been to disseminate the importance of basic design education in the current context of computational trends in architecture. The nineteenth-century context of ideas included educational reforms that placed emphasis on active learning, psychology, and hands-on experimentation with the rules ever-changing due to sensorial interactions. Looking back at the nineteenth-century origins in Ross and Dow's teaching reveals clues to a foundational core to design thinking that relates to the individual's ability to compute in the same way as design. In this way, both design and computation are challenged.

0.1 Structure of the Book

The book is divided into two parts that can be read separately or together. Part I, entitled "Early Beginnings," presents the two aforementioned educators – Denman W. Ross and Arthur W. Dow – drawing out the key aspects of their methodology for teaching foundations for design and art. Part I frames the intellectual context in which they operated and frames this from the perspective of developments in psychology in relation to arts and design, while building up an alternative background to basic design.

Part II, entitled "Looking to the Future," offers a critical look at the common perception of basic design since the Bauhaus, points out the fallacy of Pragmatism when interpreted devoid of the bodily experience, and draws out the alternative with reference to Ross and Dow's frame of psychology and Pragmatist philosophy. Part II also provides some key concepts for the content of a foundational studio curriculum today.

In Part I, Chapter 1, "Seeing Design in Art: Visions of Denman Waldo Ross" and Chapter 2, "Abstract Forms and Form Relations:

6 *Introduction*

Arthur Wesley Dow," offer an overview of Denman Ross's and Arthur Dow's particular works that have pedagogical implications. Surveying four different instances of their work, these two chapters show the emerging concepts of abstract forms and form relations in their design pedagogies. Ross's wallpaper pattern designs published in *Illustrations of Balance and Rhythm: For the Use of Students and Teachers* (Ross *et al.*, 1900) are important as they were exercises given to students. Ross's unpublished analyses of photography and painting indicate processes of abstraction. Similarly, Dow's teaching method, from his book entitled *Composition: A Series of Exercises in Art Structure for the Use of Students and Teachers* (1997 [1899]) and a collection of his unpublished personal notes, illustrate how to structure paintings with abstract guidelines. Finally, these chapters show the impact of techniques and material, especially on Dow's work, as a precursor to discussions of hands-on learning today.

Chapter 3, entitled "The Psychology for Basic Design in the Late Nineteenth Century," presents a historical and epistemological context for the concepts introduced in the previous chapters and discusses their implications as pedagogical methods. The main objective of basic design education, as it originates from this context, is the personal development of the student towards a democratic society. Sensory experiences are an active part in this development as students learn to develop their own ways to approach problems. To further articulate the dynamics of abstract form and form relations with reference to sense perception, this chapter draws attention to the notions of sagacity and changing part-whole relations that arise out of the philosophical discussions in the nineteenth century. These discussions, as well as the interest in the psychology of art at the time, provide a background to the emerging perspective to creative thinking. Finally, the chapter focuses on how Dow and Ross developed the abstract forms and relations as intellectual tools in design and used them to convey a reasoning process that varies with perception.

In Part II, Chapter 4, "The Disillusioning Pasts of Basic Design," recognizes the Pragmatist premise in the pedagogical approaches of Ross and Dow. While presenting the shortcomings of Ross and Dow's approaches, it also argues that their thinking was progressive in foreseeing the methodologies later applied to the extreme, and eventually with some failure, in the avant-garde schools, such as the Bauhaus and the VKhUTEMAS. Ross and Dow belong to a short-lived period in between the formal idealisms of the past and the twentieth century.

Chapter 5 "Computational Design Foundations" introduces what may constitute a core framework for foundational design knowledge, one that simultaneously addresses democratic creativity and technological developments in connection to the history presented in the previous chapters. This chapter underlines design thinking as a reasoning process while enunciating computing, with or without computers, as a natural component of design. Drawing parallels between the culture of hands-on learning and the culture of shape-computing, the chapter establishes a relation between the logic behind the tools and design processes at the very early stages of design education. It illustrates, through the historical example of geometric patterns and the state-of-the-art visual computation devices, how design computability provides the means to formally and explicitly talk about creative processes. Analytical modes of design thinking are useful as a means for beginning students to consciously reflect on their design thinking and become aware of their physical and visual interactions with the surroundings, the design operations, and to understand the nature of systemic and relational thinking in design processes in order to develop a sense for their processes of design.

Chapter 6, "Conclusion: Pragmatics of a Foundational Design Studio" recapitulates the pragmatist perspective to basic design education and situates within it the possibility of a reinvented basic design curriculum that is geared towards integrating notions of computation and architectural design education. Ross and Dow were active at a time that saw the emergence of Pragmatism in American philosophy. The pragmatism they practiced was psychology-driven as opposed to a technology- and market-driven pragmatism. It should be possible today to focus once again on psychology and reconstruct an understanding of basic design that embraces the personal and sensory thought processes of the novice students. This understanding of reasoning in design education in the end will reflect on how professionals thoughtfully approach parametric design, grammars, fabrication, and other tools of design technology for a better, more sustainable, and enjoyable built environment.

8 *Introduction*

Bibliography

Dow, Arthur Wesley. *Composition: A Series of Exercises in Art Structure for the Use of Students and Teachers*. Berkeley, CA: University of California Press, 1997 [1899, 1920].

Jaffee, Barbara. "Before the New Bauhaus: From Industrial Drawing to Art and Design Education in Chicago." *Design Issues*, v. 21, n. (1) (Winter, 2005), 41–62.

Martin, Marianne W. "Some American Contributions to Early Twentieth-Century Abstraction." *Arts Magazine*, v. 10, n. (54) (June 1980), 158–165.

Ross, Denman W. and Arthur W. Dow. "Architectural Education." *The Inland Architect and News Record*, v. 5, n. 37 (1901): 38.

Ross, Denman W., Edgar O. Parker, and S. Clifford Patchett. *Illustrations of Balance and Rhythm: For the Use of Students and Teachers*. Boston: W. B. Clarke Company, 1900.

Part I
Early Beginnings

1 Seeing Design in Art
Visions of Denman Waldo Ross

Denman Waldo Ross (1853–1935), a painter and a prominent art collector in late nineteenth- and early twentieth-century Boston, was among the few to start a tradition of foundational design education in America at the time. Ross taught design in the Architecture and Fine Arts Departments of Harvard University between the years 1899 and 1935, mostly in the summers. He had previously made his name as a painter, taking classes from disciples of the influential John Ruskin. His watercolor patterns earned him recognition in the American Arts and Crafts Movement. Nevertheless, his art is not published, exhibited, or discussed as widely as are his theories on design principles and teaching, culminating in works entitled *Illustrations of Balance and Rhythm* (Ross *et al.*, 1900), *Design as Science* (Ross, 1901), *A Theory of Pure Design* (Ross, 1907), and *On Drawing and Painting* (Ross, 1912). Ross's considerable contribution to the field has been through his approach to teaching art and design.

The pedagogical legacy of Denman W. Ross has mostly survived through his students who either continued teaching at higher education institutions, as Arthur Pope did at Harvard, or turned, as did Georgie O'Keefe, to practicing modern art. Art historians Marianne W. Martin (1980), Mary Ann Stankiewicz (1988), and Marie Frank (2004, 2008a, 2008b, 2011) have been among the small number of scholars who paid due attention to Ross's legacy and revealed his design theory within the context of history of art and design education in North America. Unlike these valuable historical investigations, this chapter focuses on Ross's teaching techniques and general pedagogical approach in the

12   *Early Beginnings*

context of design education and on establishing a link from 1900 to today. It is not the desire here to provide the reader with historical details on either a century-old pedagogue or on the *Zeitgeist* that he was a part of. Rather, this text aims to delineate the relevance of his teaching, craft, and theory for contemporary education in design thinking.

Ross had a unique perspective into the teaching of art. He read art critics and historians such as James Jackson Jarves, John Ruskin, and Charles Eliot Norton, he inclined towards viewing art as a product of the mind and not just through its appeal to the senses (Frank, 2008a, 74–75). This intellectual backdrop shaped an interest in Ross towards the means, the how-to, and eventually a theory of design for the arts. His positioning of the term design in front of the term art in a theory about methods is not trivial. The notions of art and design were entwined in the art education scene of the final quarter of the nineteenth century (Jaffee, 2005). As signaled in coincident discussions that took place at the time on the social role of the artist and how the character of artists is generally perceived by society (Singerman, 1999), there was a desire to redefine the terms and practice of art. Ross distinguished between the two terms and reverted to the use of the word Design, rather than Art. His motivation was possibly to emphasize that design, an element in art, can be taught. Ross stated his advocacy of the means to art, rather than what it was, in the context of art education, by claiming: "The purpose of what is called art-teaching should be the production, not of objects, but of faculties, – the faculties which being exercised will produce objects of Art, naturally, inevitably" (Ross, 1907, 193). His magnum opus, *A Theory of Pure Design* and other texts served as the answer to what those faculties might be.

In most of his lectures and writings, Ross focused on elements that make up shapes such as dots, lines, outlines of planar shapes, and color as well as the principles of balance, harmony, and rhythm. The latter group of terms resonated with the recent theories in Gestalt psychology and principles of perception at the time. Ross used these terms to deliver a method that emphasized compositional skills and knowledge. As he introduced balance, rhythm and harmony as modes of order to lay foundations for art, his motto as instructor was "We aim at Order and hope for Beauty" (Ross,

1903, 358). Order was a foundation for art which the individual would be able to later perform if the foundations were laid correctly.

In examples that neglected any stylistic association, Ross referred to arrangements of nonrepresentational forms constructed of dots, lines, and colors as pure design. The phrase "pure design," as Ross uses it, is similar to what is generally understood today in abstract design, basic design, or thematic composition. Ross assigned a utility to nonrepresentational abstract form not out of his interest in modern art but due to his attention to conveying practical knowledge about the how-to of design to his students. Although Frank (2008a, 75) points out that the "pure" in the phrase "pure design" may have been a choice influenced by Jarves who used it to refer to a quality in art lost to "anatomical dexterity" starting with sixteenth-century Tuscan painters, it may be more directly linked to the "abstract beauty of line and color" that Jarves (1861, 26) mentions while listing pure design under Choice, a point of technical merit in addition to Composition.

According to Ross, design was the epitome of the means to art. All the elements of design that he depicted brought art closer to science too. That Ross (1901) at the same time vocalized his thoughts on design being a science is significant, as evidence that art, at the turn of the century, had changed in meaning for some. Ross became interested in the process of how art came about, its principles and its controlled body of knowledge. Design was the term to embody the nub of all this. Frank (2008) reports that there is no evidence to tell us of Ross's personal interest in the developments of science such as the introduction of non-Euclidean geometries or even the theory of evolution. Both developments are often referred to in reading the avant-garde European art in the early half of the twentieth century. Ross was conservative in many aspects of his artist persona but because he was a pragmatist at heart, he was persistent about methodology in art and its teaching. This was his reformative side. Ross's interest in science was conventional. He took science to be a positivist methodology of rationalization that one can apply to design. Nonetheless, he was a part of the *Zeitgeist* surrounding the said developments in science and, as shown in Chapter 4, in that *Zeitgeist*, he had some direct interest at least in the developments in psychology which were important to the arts just as much as, if not more than, those in physics and mathematics.

14 *Early Beginnings*

1.1 Wallpaper Patterns: From Ornaments to Design

Denman W. Ross was the Professor of Design Theory at Harvard University until 1935, prior to the arrival of Walter Gropius in the USA in 1937, and of International Modernism. While endorsing a then revolutionary idea of "design as a science" in his writings, Ross was introducing a fresh approach to design education that primarily targeted the imposing aesthetic structures and timeless formalisms dominant in the field at the time. He was opposed to mindless design that followed canons. He sought instead a modern methodology to replace the traditional styles in teaching design. Although they were acquaintances who seldom worked together, he and one other visionary educator, Arthur Wesley Dow, collaboratively promoted in 1901 what Ross called "pure design" as an introductory curriculum in architectural education. Ross and Dow (1901) wrote: "the study of pure design should be preliminary to the study of art in its various and specific applications." They were partially reacting to the general misconceptions of design that it is mere decoration the aesthetics of which is handed down from a past time and commonly accepted. They explained:

> Design, as it is commonly understood, is to serve the purpose of decoration or ornament by the various arts and crafts. The teaching of design means teaching "Historic Ornament," the practice of design means following historic precedents and adapting them to modern requirements. It means doing what the public knows, understands, appreciates, wants. Design is the glass of fashion, the handmaid of commerce. In three words, it is not a fine art, as it should be. The creative imagination has very little to do with it.
>
> (ibid., 38)

It was necessary to introduce pure design in order to draw attention to a new outlook. Pure design was a conceptual instrument for the understanding and application of the underlying formal structure in designs. This would reform the conventional perception of design as ornament and open up possibilities. According to Ross, pure design referred to abstract form detached from prescribed meaning and to relations between these forms. Ross's intention was to use pure design

Seeing Design in Art: Ross 15

and form relations as tools to comprehend how the visual and other material qualities play into the design process of an individual. He proceeded to show it in his pattern designs, and his analyses of paintings and photographs where he abstracted forms and looked at form relations.

Ross published some of his wallpaper pattern designs along with his students' exercises in *Illustrations of Balance and Rhythm: For the Use of Students and Teachers* (Ross et al., 1900). There is no text to explain the illustrations and the book is only a compilation of prints, but the arrangement of prints reveals a process of design to an extent. The prints are of mono-colored wallpaper patterns that are floral-looking in character. The patterns are composed of bizarre nonfigurative shapes. The darker outlines and the blotchy shading of the interiors of these enclosed shapes suggest that they were printed on the paper. In the particular arrangement of these prints, a set of these amorphous shapes precedes each design. These shapes are presented as building blocks that are then multiplied and put together in a design. An intermediary step arranges these little shapes together in a vertically symmetric unit that repeats to form the final wallpaper pattern. Each little shape performs, in turn, as a basic element of a wallpaper pattern. This reveals the process followed in the wallpaper pattern designs. The two images on the left in Figure 1.1 show the arrangement of such prints in Ross's *Illustrations of Balance and Rhythm* in Plates 2 and 3. A set of amorphous shapes precedes each design. These units are assembled and together perform as the basic element of a wallpaper pattern. These are presented on the same plate in the book. The wallpaper pattern is then presented on the subsequent plate.

The particular three-part presentation of each wallpaper pattern print in the publication is indicative of a process showing how the wallpaper pattern designs are created under Ross's instruction. As already described above, this process starts with the set of amorphous abstract shapes. These shapes are atypical in the Modernist vocabulary of abstract forms and, instead, look almost organic. Some look like leaves, perhaps. They are then assembled creatively and together perform as the motif of a wallpaper pattern. The designed motif is repeated with vertical symmetries and off-axis rhythms in the overall wallpaper pattern as expected in such designs. The

16 Early Beginnings

Figure 1.1 Left: The arrangement of prints of wallpaper designs and their compositional parts; right: spatial relations from wallpaper designs.

Sources: Left: Ross et al. (1900), Plates 2 and 3. Right: line drawings by the author.

smaller units in the beginning, however, yield to more experimental arrangements. In the example in Figure 1.1, six shapes and multiple duplicates are organized symmetrically to fit inside the imaginary boundary of a larger onion-like shape. Some of the spatial relations here include edge and corner alignments as well as shapes or parts of shapes tucked into niches in other shapes or niches formed by groups of other shapes. These are shown in detail in the drawings on the right of Figure 1.1. The first three illustrate edge and corner alignments. The second three illustrate shapes or parts of shapes tucked into the niches in other shapes or formed by groups of other shapes. These spatial relations are not arbitrary. The designer establishes various spatial relations according to different perceptions of parts of the shapes.

Most of the units are amorphous with many features identifiable in many ways. How they come together relies more on their visual qualities in that particular context. For example, the circle sits in different niches each time, one of which is shown in Figure 1.1. Rather than being grouped with an equilateral triangle and a square as in the iconic twentieth-century basic design visual motto of basic elements, the circle in this case is explored in the context of a group of irregular shapes. Other than the formal expectations based on precedents in textile and wallpaper prints of the time, these decorative patterns do not have representational and functional qualities and are purely formal exercises. At the same time, they avoid idealized forms and form relations while simply constituting a medium to explore abstract forms. Even most of the duplicates slightly vary in size, by an extended edge, an extra curve or a trimmed end. The exercise allows for changes in shapes as well as their relations to one another.

It is not clear whether the little amorphous shapes in the examples here were appropriated from previous wallpaper designs, for example, by William Morris, or whether the students or Ross created them at that moment. The designs appeared to be Victorian damask where smaller and meaningless shapes come together to form motifs that resemble quatrefoil, bi-convex ellipses, or kite shapes. Illustrations in *A Theory of Pure Design* display similar shapes which Ross constructs in the course of the text using commonplace principles of harmony, rhythm, and balance. *A Theory of Pure Design* can be taken in parts as the instruction set for constructing shapes that can be used in these types of wallpaper designs. In that book, Ross (1907) shows how to construct various shapes, and eventually designs, out of parts. Figure 1.2 shows a variety of these shapes from *A Theory of Pure Design*, constructed out of points arranged in a gradient along a curve, various arcs lined up according to their tangents and normals, and shapes composed of other curves. He mostly relies on visual criteria.

As for the origin of the wallpaper design units seven years prior to *A Theory of Pure Design*, there is no indication that the shapes were constructed carefully and intentionally. The shapes in the patterns are not symbols, and neither are they marks from brush strokes. Floral figures in Owen Jones's ornaments catalogued in 1856 may have been common precursors (Stankiewicz, 1988, 84). Still, Ross's use of these seems to parallel the intent to have unconventional figures that are difficult to deal with at the abstract level. These shapes are abstract motifs that transform natural forms such as petals, leaves, and stems but serve the same purpose. The

Figure 1.2 Some elements of Pure Design.
Source: Ross (1907), pp. 25, 40, 41, 46, 65.

18 *Early Beginnings*

level of abstraction resulting in the unfamiliarity of forms sets a distance between the students and the forms, so that they dismiss their biases and worry about establishing new and surprising relations between the forms. Without any concerns as to what the units are, these exercises focus on how one puts them together.

Moreover, there is little precision in how the shapes are drawn or printed. Formal features that are taken into account change from one end of the design to the other. Rules are not decipherable because they are context-specific and alter from design to design. The designs in Figure 1.3 share the leaf-like figure and the flame-like figure (with circle and square in it) but relate them to one another differently in the designs.

In another series of examples (Figure 1.4), a core set of little shapes is used in three different designs, the first by Ross and the remaining two by different students. Again, in each, shared units are used in different contexts. Their relations among one another and to other shapes vary greatly between the three designs. Ross does not prescribe any rules to his students in how to arrange them. Only the spatial relations applied are similar to those given earlier and where edges or corners align or shapes are tucked into niches formed by others. In Figure 1.4 three different designs are built from one vocabulary.

As mentioned earlier, Ross uses comparable shapes in *A Theory of Pure Design* to illustrate the general organizational principles of harmony, rhythm, and balance. But these principles are vague because

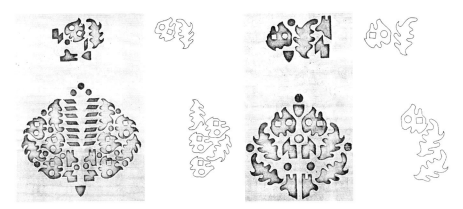

Figure 1.3 Details from Ross *et al.* (1900), Plates 1 and 2.
Note: Line drawings by the author.

Figure 1.4 Details from Ross *et al.* (1900), Plates 7, 8, and 9.
Note: Emphases by the author.
Source: Ross et al. (1900).

they are general, and do not explicitly guide these exercises. There is no visual evidence of how more detailed rules are developed and applied in wallpaper designs. Ross's motive seems to be leaving that to the students.

Additionally, these exercises also allow the students to understand dynamic part–whole relations. Designs created with small units are units in a bigger whole of the wallpaper design. And overall pattern elements resemble some of the smaller units as shown in the first two examples given in Figure 1.5. The design on the far left shows how the contour of a pattern design resembles one of the smaller units used in another pattern design second from the left in Figure 1.5. It can be said that the pattern exercises allow the students to understand dynamic part–whole relations as shapes are used at different levels of the design. Furthermore, as two separate patterns are overlapped in the image third from the left, some of the units are cut, or modified into new shapes. These new shapes are used as units in other designs, for example, in the image in the far right. Parts of shapes were also used as units. Two separate patterns are

Figure 1.5 Details from Ross *et al.* (1900), Plates 10, 6, 22, and 6.
Note: Emphases by the author.
Source: Ross *et al.* (1900).

20 Early Beginnings

overlapped in the third design whereas a part of the unit that is compromised in the overlap is used as a unit in the design on the far right.

Ross shows in *A Theory of Pure Design* that the combinatorial arrangements in the designs can overlap and create new spatial relations. The third image from the left in Figure 1.5 illustrates an overlapping spatial relation between two patterns of a wallpaper design, while their parts also engage in spatial relationships as specified before. As shown in Figure 1.6, part of one pattern encases a part of the other. This all indicates that these exercises go beyond combining given sets of shapes as students explore emerging shapes and relations at different levels.

There is one other point in looking closely at the wallpaper examples. Among Ross's personal notes, there are a few hand-drawn patterns similar to the wallpaper patterns discussed above. A couple of them illustrate Ross's use of a background grid in establishing forms and relations between the forms. The grid is an organizational means for Ross. Some of the grids are orthogonal whereas others have introduced triangles. Distances, symmetries and repetitions as well as the extrusions of the parts are all based on the verticals and horizontals of the grid. The three examples in Figure 1.7 show an orthogonal guide to soft forms and planes of orthogonal and triangular guidelines for designs. For the design on the far right, Ross's handwriting questions whether the form is a bird or a fish, indicative of a mental and visual experimentation with possibilities of the grid while the hand draws in its guidance.

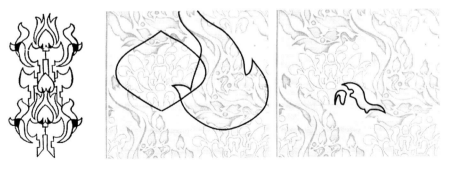

Figure 1.6 Detail from Ross (1907). The exercises go beyond combining given sets of shapes as students explore various relations between shapes at different levels.

Note: Emphases by the author.
Source: Ross (1907), p. 124.

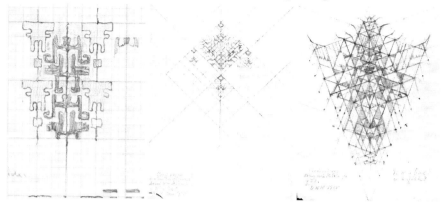

Figure 1.7 From left to right: Detail from geometric sketches with shading, undated. Sources: Denman Waldo Ross Study Materials, box 34. Harvard Art Museums Archives, Harvard University, Cambridge, MA; "Coordination in a System of Squares: Drawn Within Triangles of 90°, 45°, 45°" drawing, 1925. Denman Waldo Ross Study Materials, box 34. Harvard Art Museums Archives, Harvard University, Cambridge, MA; "Coordination: drawn with the triangle of V8,"1925. Denman Waldo Ross Study Materials, box 34. Harvard Art Museums Archives, Harvard University, Cambridge, MA.

Guideline grids are expected in regular designs such as wallpaper patterns. Another plate among Ross's personal notes depicts a floral pattern on a triangular grid as shown in Figure 1.8. However, this one, being triangular, hints at the use of different guideline geometries to adjust distances, symmetries and repetitions. Here, Ross uses a triangular grid similar to that of Hardesty G. Maratta to organize a pattern. Because patterns are repetitious by nature, the use of grids for organizational purposes is not surprising.

Ross was acquainted with designer Hardesty G. Maratta, who owned a design company that produced and distributed grid papers in the mid-1910s. These design papers were significant because their grid was triangular for the announced purpose of serving designers and artists. Maratta must have thought that designers would appreciate the dynamics of the equilateral triangle better than the square. Ross (1923) certainly did, as he wrote "easier to get good compositions with triangles than rectangles." It is possible that Ross distributed these papers to his students for drawing exercises. On the right of Figure 1.8 is another plate, drawn and sent to Ross by Maratta himself, possibly to demonstrate the use of

22 Early Beginnings

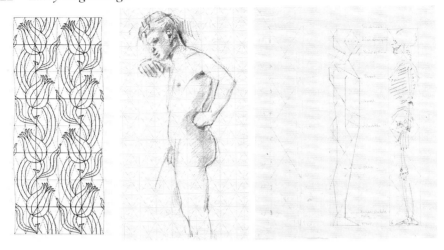

Figure 1.8 Detail from geometric floral design, undated.

Sources: Denman Waldo Ross Study Materials, box 34. Harvard Art Museums Archives, Harvard University, Cambridge, MA; Pencil sketch of a male nude in profile, undated. Denman Waldo Ross Study Materials, box 34. Harvard Art Museums Archives, Harvard University, Cambridge, MA; Geometric sketch of human skeleton, drawn by H.G. Maratta, undated. Denman Waldo Ross Study Materials, box 34. Harvard Art Museums Archives, Harvard University, Cambridge, MA.

the design paper. Maratta's design paper is unique as it introduces a triangular grid rather than a square one. The exchange between the two men anticipated Ross's later practices that utilize abstract lines as active guidelines in design. How Ross used and furthered the idea of connecting the figural composition with abstract lines will be explained in detail in the forthcoming section.

Ross also superimposed the Maratta grid on paintings by other artists. Marie Frank (2008a) cites one such instance where Ross superimposes a regular Maratta grid on a reproduction of Peter Paul Rubens's *Descent from the Cross*. The significance in Ross's superimpositions as such is that in most of this work, Ross was trying to expand the utility of triangular guidelines. Mostly, his artistic investigation is not just in a regulated grid but in a controlled system that he, as the artist, develops systematically and to a certain extent freely. In the *Descent from the Cross*, we see that the lines of the grid start to disappear selectively as precursor to Ross's more typical analyses.

Seeing Design in Art: Ross 23

1.2 Tracing Lines on Photography: Organization of Forms

Denman Ross developed his educational methods of design over the course of thirty years that followed the initiation of his theory of pure design. Following his introduction to the Maratta grid and his use of orthogonal grids as background to pattern designs, he uniquely used grid lines to analyze paintings and photography in the late 1920s. At a first glance, his analyses of paintings resemble conventional ones, of mostly classical paintings, executed to represent how various figures are compositionally linked in a picture.In a few of these analyses, Ross examines Michelangelo's compositions as seen in Figure 1.9. His visual analyses are either done by drawing lines drawn on a tracing paper, which he places on the image, or by directly drawing on the image with chalk or crayon. Lines form triangles and thus mark the outlines of triangles that connect to one another at corners or overlap in area. Ross draws a triangular grid similar to Maratta's over a reproduction of a Michelangelo fresco in the Sistine Chapel in Rome. The grid differs from Maratta's design paper, first, because it is constructed after the fact, in analysis, and, second, because it is not complete to the ends.

In the margins of his analyses, Ross often indicates numeric details about his applied method for that analysis. He spells out which right triangle and the corresponding rectangle is in use. He identifies triangles through the nomenclature of roots. In the example above, the explanation for his formal analyses is "with triangle of √4" referring to the elemental right triangle in the analysis with the 2:1 ratio of hypotenuse to one side. A triangle of √4 is a right triangle where the sides are multiples of 1, √3 and 2 consecutively. "No use of reciprocal" means he does not rotate the triangle. Except for the one referred to by the question mark at the top, all triangles have the long side upright. Ross often puts question marks in these analysis to designate his exploration of alternative setups. All triangles in this particular analysis together form the equilateral triangular grid that Maratta also popularized in his design papers.

Since Ross draws long lines, which he refers to as diagonals, rather than individual triangles, it is not immediately clear why he announces the basic unit as the triangle. Through the totality of his writings, however, it is clear that he is predisposed to consider that we construct

Figure 1.9 Geometric analysis with triangle of √4 of figure from Sistine Chapel ceiling by Michelangelo, undated.

Source: Denman Waldo Ross Study Materials, box 31. Harvard Art Museums Archives, Harvard University, Cambridge, MA.

Seeing Design in Art: Ross 25

shapes out of basic elements such as lines, in line with the narrative in *A Theory of Pure Design* exemplified in Figure 1.1. In the catalogue for an exhibition, Ross (1923) explains his process meticulously. He describes looking at his subject and deciding which diagonal would be suitable to start with. Drawing diagonals one after the other in a sequence, he carefully conducts towards a system of right triangles (ibid., 4–5). What he creates is an incomplete grid, in connection to the previous grid examples he has either used or been exposed to. There are analyses where he frames the diagonals by squares or rectangles, as in the photographs to come later on in the section, and he often refers to the square or rectangle of a triangle in the figure caption. Nonetheless, Ross is not interested in constructing a grid to homogenize the form relations in the entire painting. He focuses on local relations and he is willing to flex the structure of the grid, for example, by using reciprocals of the same triangle in the analysis of another Michelangelo wall painting shown in Figure 1.10. Ross constructs his abstract lines differently than Maratta's uniform grid. The basic unit is still a √4 right triangle but Ross modifies its scale and orientation as he places it on the image.

In Figure 1.10, Ross breaks down the grid to a system of varying scales according to the picture. He focuses mostly on the face area with smaller triangles. His selective use of lines indicates how he utilizes the concept of a grid. Unlike holistic geometry in analyses by others, Ross's lines display his perception of the images in the painting and explore the different form relations they may offer. They do not impose an external order on it. The schema to emerge at the end is not a simplistic diagram of the painting that claims to give a mathematical explanation for its composition. Rather, it is a plane of diagonals relating to one another in an experiment to discover abstract form relations.

Among Ross's notes at the Harvard University Art Museums Archives, we find examples of conventional analyses that aspire to the beauty and harmony in nature and superimpose finished geometries on images of complete designs. One is of an image of the Renaissance structure of Loggia del Consiglio from fifteenth-century Verona. The front façade drawing of the historical building is overlain with a geometric construction of a large circle, a star of David and a vesica piscis that overlap and fit into it perfectly. It is not clear that this is an analysis by Ross himself. Ross's approach is usually

26 *Early Beginnings*

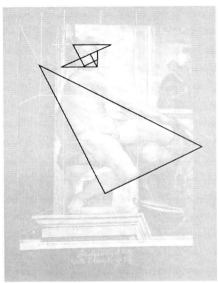

Figure 1.10 Design analysis with triangle of √4 of figure from Sistine Chapel ceiling by Michelangelo, undated.
Note: Dark line drawings by the author.
Source: Denman Waldo Ross Study Materials, box 31. Harvard Art Museums Archives, Harvard University, Cambridge, MA.

not this type of idealistic analyses. The geometry that Ross uses in other analyses such as the Michelangelo examples interacts with changing parts of the image. The geometry in this image, instead, is finished and superimposed on the façade. This example situates Ross's work for us in an intriguing way. Such diagrams surely have influenced Ross, but he develops a different approach in the analyses he conducts. He moves away from the rigidity of a finished and idealized diagram to explore form relations in unfinished ones. His motivation differs from romanticizing about geometric explanations for classical forms. For example, he goes out of his way to indicate that his choice of geometry is personal. In the same exhibition catalogue mentioned earlier, he explains that the equilateral triangle is his favorite shape and the "right angled triangle is wonderful as module" (Ross, 1923, 2). He must be thinking, along the same lines as Maratta, that the triangle offers more possibilities if it is the base for a grid.

The background grid for wallpaper patterns prompts a simple way to think about form relations. Its triangular unit in Ross's succeeding analyses of painting and photography works similarly. The triangle represents an abstract form relation and has a smaller number of components to deal with. The difference in this case is that its instances connect to varying parts in the image. In this sense, Ross's picture analyses rise above the shortcoming of a grid in understanding dynamic relations. The angles and the scale of the grid change, along with the relations they prescribe. Ross uses systems of triangles not because he believes that they truly represent the relations of the images, but because it is a way for him to understand how the simple relations between the triangles translate into different contexts.

These triangles and grids resemble an older tradition of drawing that we see in the thirteenth-century engineer-architect Villard D'Honnecourt's sketches, as well as the studies of Ross's contemporary, Jay Hambidge. Hambidge developed the notion of dynamic symmetry as a technical structure for the creative arts. Incidentally, his writings refer to D'Honnecourt to show that designers in the medieval past have used guides to understand and create form relations (Hambidge, 1960 [1932], 5). D'Honnecourt, like Ross, looks at the relationships between forms at an abstract level. But again, Ross does not idealize any of his abstract forms. Without holding onto a general aesthetic preference, he develops a better understanding of organizational relations and his study carries more awareness of the flexibility of experimentation. There are sketches where D'Honnecourt overlays geometries on facial figures. One example is a diagonal square that is divided into eight triangles and overlain on an orthogonal grid of squares superimposed on a drawing of a male face (Hahnloser, 1972 [1935], Plate 38). Another is the five-pointed star drawn on a drawing of the face of an old male (Hahnloser, 1972 [1935], Plate 36). In one unique example, D'Honnecourt couples together a large and a small triangle that actually fit in a sketch of an adult holding a child in their lap (Hahnloser, 1972 [1935], Plate 37). The larger triangle corresponds to the adult and the smaller one to the child, as to distinguish the differently sized instances of the same compositional element. The first of these three sketches resembles a few of Ross's analyses with the exception that it is a square grid. Ross almost always uses a triangle grid. Again unlike Ross's unfinished diagrams, D'Honnecourt's other two sketches display self-contained geometries. Ross's analyses show open-ended grids and construction of the geometries.

28 *Early Beginnings*

Additionally, D'Honnecourt's sketches tend towards displaying symbolic meaning, for example, the pentagon in the second example described above. Painting analysis done in Johannes Itten's Berlin School in 1932 comes closer to Ross's organization of the picture plane as it is also detached from symbolic meaning. In an analysis of Memling's portrait of Willem Moreel by a student at Itten's design school in Berlin, various lines are drawn on the canvas. They are all at seemingly random angles. One passes tangentially to the rather straight outline of one cheek whereas three others align respectively with the collar, the afro, and the nasal bone. Two vertical lines match the columns in the background that frame the portrait while the only horizontal line passes through the two eyes and is aligned with the horizon line in the back. There seem to be eight lines in total. Almost all of these lines are part of a right triangle. Itten (1963, 128) explains this analysis in the original figure caption: "Its purpose was to study the geometric-constructive organization of the picture plane. The guides, found by the student, connect points of accent and reinforce the structure." Ross's work anticipates this later study in many ways, and even shows more "constructive organization" because it employs a more willful and controlled investigation of the guides.

A few of the painting analyses by Ross are of natural scenes. That he does not confine his analyses to classical paintings is further evidence of his attempts to understand form relations. As he overlays his grid lines, he pays attention to compositional arrangements and uses the lines in a selective and dynamic way. Figure 1.11 provides two examples. In the top row, rather than looking at how the composition fits into the geometry of $\sqrt{4}$ triangles, Ross observes its elements in relation to one another, such as where the break in the clouds is, and how this relates to the direction of the storm as well as the general framing of the image. The other analysis in the bottom row illustrates similar observations as the one in the top row. The trees mimic the rhythm of rock slopes and the composition brings the two systems together. Ross simplifies and abstracts how he sees the formal arrangement.

A larger set of Ross's analyses is of photographs, where he additionally has control over the content as he is the photographer and he looks at how he can manipulate the formal arrangement.

Figure 1.11 Top row: "The Jetty of Calais" by J.M.W. Turner with diagonals of √4, rectangle of √2, 3 √4 rectangles approximately, undated; bottom row: "Little Devil's Bridge" by J.M.W. Turner with chalk lines drawn with the triangle of √4, undated.

Note: Dark line drawings by the author.
Sources: Denman Waldo Ross Study Materials, box 31. Harvard Art Museums Archives, Harvard University, Cambridge, MA; Denman Waldo Ross Study Materials, box 31. Harvard Art Museums Archives, Harvard University, Cambridge, MA.

Some of his photography work was exhibited along with his paintings in 1923. However, there is not an extensive publication of these analyses.

Ross's choice to analyze photographs seems curious. Most of them are portraits of young male models. Similar to the Classical and Renaissance imagery, the reasoning behind this might be in connection to an ideal of Beauty. Ross contemplates a little more on this point of beauty in *A Theory of Pure Design*:

> I refrain from any reference to Beauty as a principle of Design. It is not a principle, but an experience ... While I am quite unable to give any definition or explanation of Beauty, I know where to look for it.

30   *Early Beginnings*

The Beautiful is revealed, always, so far as I know, in the forms of Order, in the modes of Harmony, of Balance, or of Rhythm.

(1907, 4)

The analyses might have been for understanding the abstract rules underlying the classical notion of "Beauty." Nevertheless, as the selected examples below will show, despite the classical poses their subjects sometimes adopt, photographs are still products of a different realism than that of the Michelangelo paintings or the idealism in Hambidge's Greek meander analyses. Therefore it is debatable but possible to ignore the choice of subject matter in the photographs and accept that they are simply portraits. Ross starts his analyses with diagonals that relate to certain features in the photographs. In the analysis above, the attached painting hints at what compositional features Ross is looking at. The profiles in the two images have similarities. The lines redrawn in the image on the right in Figure 1.12 are possibly the first diagonals. Based on the spatial relation these initial lines produce – defined with the angle between the lines – Ross constructs a system. The system repeats the same relation in different scales, rotations, and symmetries. The composition of diagonals correlates with the figural composition in the photograph.

Even if rarely, and given the size of the image overall, reluctantly, Ross occasionally attempts to modify the actual image based on his observations with the abstract lines – his intellectual tool. There are attempts at possible changes in the figural composition based on decisions at the abstract level. The detail in Figure 1.13 shows one of these instances where Ross is considering moving the hand of the subject to fit a different triangle in the system he constructs. He reconsiders the position of the hand in relation to the other. Note the similar triangles contemplated for both hands. This indicates Ross's interest in using the lines for more than analysis.

These are not pleas for aesthetic principles but attempts to develop ways to construct designs and at the same time to understand these ways. Ross shows how, at different levels of abstraction, he wishes to apply principles of composition. Relations are easier to see with simpler shapes. This could easily have been his pedagogical method as well. For Ross, the grid in the background and the diagonals instigate a

Figure 1.12 Photograph of young man in profile with geometric analysis and inset of "Ritratto di Lionello d'Este" by Vittore Pisano, undated.
Note: Dark line drawings by the author.
Source: Denman Waldo Ross Study Materials, box 30. Harvard Art Museums Archives, Harvard University, Cambridge, MA.

learning of how to relate simple forms in simple contexts. Ross (1907, 77) wrote that "the value of any composition lies in the number of orderly connections which it shows." This was picked up on by Fry (1920 [1909], 21) who appreciated the abstract quality that Ross introduced in *A Theory of Pure Design* for the purposes of clearly identifying instances of order such as unity in a "closely woven geometrical texture."

Ross's theory of pure design finds correlation in his own works of photography as composition and of wallpaper patterns from an earlier time. We see the application of a methodology and a keen eye in the arrangement of shapes for the wallpapers, first, with focus on immediate form relations, then with focus on underlying guidelines that bring forms together in a holistic composition, as in the examples on grids. The method further develops into how the designer manipulates the guiding system to benefit

Figure 1.13 Photograph of young man seated in 3/4 pose with geometric analysis drawn with the XM triangle, undated.

Source: Denman Waldo Ross Study Materials, box 30. Harvard Art Museums Archives, Harvard University, Cambridge, MA.

from it as an instrument to relate forms in an overall composition, a common theme to all the examples cited in this book.

Bibliography

Frank, Marie. "Emil Lorch: Pure Design and American Architectural Education." *Journal of Architectural Education*, v. 57, n. 4 (May 2004): 28–41.

Frank, Marie. "Denman Waldo Ross and the Theory of Pure Design." *American Art*, v. 22, n. 3 (2008a), 72–89.

Frank, Marie. "The Theory of Pure Design and American Architectural Education in the Early Twentieth Century." *Journal of the Society of Architectural Historians*, v. 67, n. 2 (2008b), 248–273.

Frank, Marie. *Denman Ross and American Design Theory*. Lebanon, NH: University Press of New England, 2011.

Fry, Roger. "An Essay in Aesthetics." *New Quarterly*, 2 (April 1909), 171–190. Reprinted in *Vision and Design*. London: Chatto and Windus, 1920, pp. 16–38.

Hahnloser, Hans R. *Villard de Honnecourt: Kritische Gesamtausgabe des Bauhüttenbuches ms. fr 19093 der Pariser Nationalbibliothek*. Graz: Akademische Druck- u. Verlagsanstalt, 1972 [1935].

Hambidge, Jay. *Practical Applications of Dynamic Symmetry*. New York: The Devin-Adair Company, 1960 [1932].

Itten, Johannes. *Design and Form: The Basic Course at the Bauhaus*. Trans. John Maass. New York: Reinhold Publishing Corporation, 1963.

Jaffee, Barbara. "Before the New Bauhaus: From Industrial Drawing to Art and Design Education in Chicago." *Design Issues*, v. 21, n. 1 (2005): 41–62.

Jarves, James Jackson. *Art Studies: The "Old Masters" of Italy; Painting*. New York: Derby and Jackson, 1861.

Martin, Marianne W. "Some American Contributions to Early Twentieth-century Abstraction." *Arts Magazine*, v. 10, n. 54 (June 1980): 158–165.

Ross, Denman W. "Design as a Science." *Proceedings of the American Academy of Arts and Sciences*, v. 21, n. 36 (March 1901): 357–374.

Ross, Denman W. Address on Design: Public Exercises at the Dedication of the Memorial Hall. Given at Rhode Island School of Design. Tuesday, November 24, 1903. Biographical and general information relating to Denman Waldo Ross, ca. 1880–ca. 1935. HUG 1753.400. Harvard University Archives.

Ross, Denman W. *A Theory of Pure Design: Harmony, Balance, Rhythm*. Boston: Houghton, Mifflin Company, 1907.

Ross, Denman W. *On Drawing and Painting*. Boston: Houghton Mifflin Company, 1912.

Ross, Denman W. *Experiments in Drawing and Painting*. New York: The Century Association of New York, Exhibition, November 1923.

34 *Early Beginnings*

Ross, Denman W. and Arthur W. Dow. "Architectural Education." *The Inland Architect and News Record*, v. 5, n. 37 (June 1901): 38.

Ross, Denman W., Edgar O. Parker, and S. Clifford Patchett. *Illustrations of Balance and Rhythm: For the Use of Students and Teachers*. Boston: W. B. Clarke Company, 1900.

Singerman, Howard. *Art Subjects: Making Artists in the American University*. Berkeley, CA: University of California Press, 1999.

Stankiewicz, Mary Ann. "Form, Truth and Emotion: Transatlantic Influences on Formalist Aesthetics." *Journal of Art & Design Education*, v. 1, n. 7 (1988).

2 Abstract Forms and Form Relations
Arthur Wesley Dow

Arthur Wesley Dow (1857–1922), an American artist and influential art educator at the turn of the twentieth century, gave a talk to the Kindergarten Association in Philadelphia on February 15, 1906. This talk was among many that he gave over the years as part of the advocacy for widespread art education. Dow was a prominent figure in the American arts and crafts culture with his New England landscapes, woodcut prints, and applied arts. He taught painting as composition first at Ipswich, MA, starting from before the turn of the century, also at Pratt Institute between 1895–1904, and later in Teachers College at Columbia University in New York between 1908–1922. His pedagogical influence persisted with *Composition*, his book on the basics of painting and applied arts which was first published in 1899.

In the 1906 talk, or at least in its draft form as we know it from the archives, Dow identified two misconceptions as to the nature of fine art. One was that art is representation and that there is an expectation for art to have a communicative accuracy just as we rely on grammar to ensure common understandings in language (Dow, 1906). Contrarily, Dow was interested in the richness of different interpretations in art and relies on abstraction as the means to art as such. His clear stance was that painting is not to imitate nature but instead should represent some aspects of it and with inaccuracy. In another lecture, the first one of his famous *Talks on Appreciation of Art*, Dow stated: "the artist does not teach us to see facts: he teaches us to feel harmonies …" (Dow, 1915). Harmonies referred to the coherent relations between the elements of art or design as envisioned and manifested by the artist. Maybe not the

36   *Early Beginnings*

feeling, but certainly the seeing and the constructing of harmonies were a part of the teaching that Dow practices. For instance, he encouraged his students to paint natural scenes from memory. In an interview entitled "An Explanation of Certain Methods of Art Teaching," he claimed: "To set [the students] to drawing from nature as a means of studying art is philosophically and pedagogically wrong" (Dow, n.d.). According to Dow, looking on and imitating a natural scene were more "picture-writing" or "literature" than art as he wanted to teach it. Instead, if drawing from memory, students refrain from trying to capture the truth but are forced to express varying perceptions of nature.

One other misconception as to the nature of art, according to Dow, was that it is directly linked to science. Although it is not clear what Dow considered science, it may well be that he took his fellow artists' take as reference. When he drafted his talk, Dow might have been thinking of the ideas in *Design as Science*, a text that his fellow Arts and Crafts artist and educator Denman Waldo Ross wrote and published in 1901. Ross was interested in revealing and developing systematic procedures for creating art, and in his fervor to discard the customs of art as a trade distant from rational ways as much as possible, he coined the term "design as science." Dow and Ross were not inimical to one another. They shared an interest in developing a methodological core to design teaching. They are known to have worked together and but also to have been critical of the other at different times. Although Dow (1906) dismissed the idea of assigning mechanical components to design, and to apply a set formula as taking the easy way out, and it may have been Ross who was his target here, Ross and Dow are not very different in the degree of rationalization they proposed for art. They both introduced a method of abstraction to guide certain formal arrangements to answer to principles of composition such as harmony, rhythm, and balance. We understand that Dow may have just been cautious towards a reliance on timeless canons. This chapter attests to the similarity as much as the difference in Dow's approach to education focusing on abstraction with regard to that of Ross.

Dow's preferred pedagogy was the use of some – indistinct – guiding principles and the individual's experience of the relevant phenomenon before drawing. One guiding principle was visual abstraction. Dow's abstractions helped his pedagogical ideas in that the student first experiences the form relations in the abstract frameworks, right then and there, contained within the example. This to a certain extent allowed the student to apply similar experiences later in other, more sophisticated or complex situations.

Dow's concept of abstraction empowered the students to experiment with the basic relations, so that they could come up with their own experiences. This tied in with his answer to the problem of art being misconceived as a science: copying nature becomes mechanical if practiced as a teaching method, and is only a search for Truth. Dow was critical of conventional ways of teaching art and academicism. He emphasized his perspective against following a formula, again and again, in reports about his classes as well as in his text for an exhibition at the conference of Fine Arts and Industrial Arts (1914), his sixth and last lecture in the course entitled "~~Modern~~ [originally scratched] Landscape Painting" given to the Board of Education (Dow, 1905) and in his "Talks on Appreciation of Art, No. IV, Color" (Dow, 1916, 15).

2.1 Abstractions: Structuring Images

Arthur Wesley Dow's attentiveness to abstraction and using it as an instrumental guide to composition comes across strongly in his magnum opus, *Composition: A Series of Exercises in Art Structure for the Use of Students and Teachers*, where he demonstrated that simple form relations underlie compositions despite what the forms are. In two drawings entitled "Principles of Composition III," he chose to show the concept through the abstract forms of horizontal and vertical lines (Dow, 1997 [1899, 1920], 83). One of the drawings is a rectangle divided by vertical and horizontal lines and the second one is a simple landscape, fitted in a rectangular frame of the same size, displaying a black line drawing of two trees with shrubs in the background. The vertical lines in the first drawing match the placements of the tree trunks in the second and the horizontal lines match the horizon line and the horizontally spreading branches of the trees. The two drawings share the same kind of relations between parts. Simultaneously, the first drawing of straight lines is a visual abstraction of the second one. The two drawings match perfectly when overlain on tracing paper.

38   *Early Beginnings*

Dow's contemporary, Denman Waldo Ross experimented with overlaying abstract lines on already existing work to theorize about the instrumentality of these lines for compositional organization. Dow showed these lines as a constructive tool from the beginning of the design process. While Ross was analysing existent compositions in terms of form relations and was experimenting with simpler forms to take these relations to different contexts, Dow's illustration established a similar connection between the landscape sketch and the line arrangements, even though they are not physically overlapping in Dow's book. At the same time, it emphasized that these simple lines display the structural relations to construct this painting. Dow's approach was parallel to Ross's in principle, especially to Ross's use of the grid for wallpaper patterns. Nonetheless, Dow's work lacked the rich experimentation Ross allowed himself in the picture analyses regarding what various structural relations might be. On the other hand, unlike Ross's inarticulate aspiration for a composition in the analyses, Dow used abstract form relations as guidelines to create original compositions. For Dow, abstract guidelines were at the same time the abstraction of the compositional idea. The lines divided up the canvas according to initial decisions on delineating figure and ground ratios, where to place components of the painting and how to frame the scene.

Dow's abstractions worked pedagogically. He referred to abstract lines, first, to show that relations exist at all levels, and, second, to construct paintings from those relations. In almost all of the exercises given in *Composition*, he encouraged his readers to start by thinking simply in this way. His actual students later reflected back on experiencing a similar instruction. The American avant-garde painter Max Weber was a student of Dow before returning to Paris in 1907 and getting involved with the Cubists. Moffat (1977) cites Weber's description of a class with Dow:

> [Dow] would come into class and make an unbounded drawing of trees and hills, or perhaps a winding road against the sky. Then he would ask the class to copy the drawing freely and enclose it in a rectangle, to make a horizontal picture or a vertical, as they chose, and to make whatever changes necessary to fit the drawing to the

Abstract Forms and Form Relations: Dow 39

frame which they had selected, to balance the drawing by making less foreground, or more sky, to change the masses what not.

(Weber, cited in Moffat 1977, 82)

Drawings produced in the way described by Weber are numerous in *Composition*. In one set of drawings, Dow presents five alternative framings of the same landscape (1997 [1899, 1920], 104). A group of trees are framed in each drawing by different-sized rectangular boundaries. One is more vertically elongated, and another one is more horizontally spread. The sizing of the trees is almost the same in all five but the captured scene differs based on how much of it fits in the frame. The emphases on features also change. We see more trunks in one and more of the horizon line in another as Dow experiments with the idea of variance in composition based on form relations. The framing of the landscape, and dependently, the compositional structure vary. Nature is observed not as an ideal, but in representations that change. If we were to superimpose horizontal and vertical lines on these five drawings, the number of vertical and horizontal lines would more or less be the same but the ratios of distances in between them and how they divide up the frame would be different. This parametric manipulation of proportions of the elements in the picture frame, resembles D'Arcy Thompson's illustrations of transformations. The arrangement of elements inside the frame changes along with the frame. In an exercise Dow (1997 [1899, 1920], 106) gave this instruction: to find the "best way of setting the subject upon canvas or paper, arrange this in rectangles of varying shape, some nearly square, others tall, others long and narrow horizontally." Dow's intention to structure a painting started from the framing. He explicitly described how one should try out multiple versions to develop a sense of composition: "To discover the best arrangement, and to get the utmost experience in line and space composition, the landscape should be set into several boundaries of differing proportions"(ibid., 107).

John La Farge, another American painter and contemporary of Dow, talked of "rules for art" (1908, 36) and emphasized the significance of how an image is framed: "The frame decides the question – for there is no frame in nature" (cited in Adams, 1987). Similarly, Dow was interested not so much in the structure of nature but how to structure its various

40 *Early Beginnings*

representations. He pursued this idea in developing a system of abstraction demonstrated by horizontal and vertical lines. And the choices in how a landscape is framed fit within this system of abstraction for vertical and horizontal lines. Contrary to Ross's analyses, that were usually open-ended and incomplete systems of lines, Dow's illustrations displayed line arrangements that were self-contained and premeditated simple compositions.

When Denman Ross executed his analyses, he did not think of this minimalist formalism as a new style but rather as a tool in understanding the design/process. He did not open the aesthetics in his work to discussion as a stylistic issue at all. He assigned peculiar shapes in the wallpaper designs and used peculiar triangles in his analyses as he liked. He also proposed that somebody else would have different preferences. Dow, on the other hand, in his abstractions, was more or less influenced by the minimalist aesthetics of Japanese art, along with the production techniques that have an effect on it. Marie Frank (2008) accounts for Dow's stylistic legacy in design education. It is common that the appeal of minimalist forms, even if they were originally created to serve as guidelines rather than as composition, results in their misconception as aesthetic manifests. Nonetheless, Dow's approach, like Ross's, was first and foremost significant from a pedagogical point of view in its focus on the simplification of spatial relations and their representation in the form of horizontal and vertical lines. Dow encouraged his students to think about composition through abstract guidelines and empowered them in manipulating form relations systematically and with control.

2.2 Techniques, Methods, and Materials: Structuring Processes

Simultaneously using structural lines, Dow also wrote about the material and tools used in painting. He described various kinds of brushes, ink, and other painting tools, as he wanted the students to understand the qualities that come from these. He discussed the ink marks left on the paper if a brush is held differently. But more importantly, Dow achieved abstraction, similar to that with lines, through his choice of technique. His notion of "notan," which is explained as harmony of dark and light, came from woodcut printing that he appropriated and mastered in Japan.

Abstract Forms and Form Relations: Dow 41

The influence of technique is even more evident in Dow's woodcut prints. Aside from contextualizing aesthetics, technique helped Dow conceptualize abstraction and abstract form. Woodcut printing resulted in a minimization of details as well as the homogeneity of color and shade in individual surface areas. Dow's woodcut prints were another tool to abstract forms. Most of his posters illustrated the abstract quality of the image which was prepared using this technique (Green and Poesch, 1999, 16).

The minimalism, suggested in Dow's posters and woodcut paintings, gave rise to the idea of notan exhibited in other exercises. In addition to showing different ways of using black and white contrast to depict scenes, these indicated abstraction of forms to zones of shade and light. Dow achieved formal abstraction in black and white (Dow, 1997 [1899, 1920], 128). He experimented with producing copies of the same woodcut with different allocations of black ink and color. Several series have alternating colors, even textures, and as an end result, different contrasts or expressive atmosphere. For instance, in a series of three woodcuts of the same dory, he tries out the sky, the background coast and the reflection of the boat in black, whereas in the second one everything but the reflection of the boat is black. And in the third one, only the water and the background coast are black.

Using stencils achieved the same kind of abstraction. The stencil did not have the kind of hand control that there is with the brush. For the ink to have the desired effect, lines needed to be continuous and forms needed to be abstract, displaying new relations proposed by the painter. For example, a tree in front of a house in the shadow blended in with the house simply because of light–shade criteria. Material and techniques became a part of the thought process, in the sense that they shaped the relationships to observe and represent. Components of the painting were abstracted to a simple relationship that students could experience and experiment with. The way stencils were punched affected the ink marks on the paper. It was a different tool than the pen or the brush. The ink marks were controlled by predefined cuts in the paper (Green and Poesch, 1999, 68).

Also in the concept of notan, lines were upgraded from being boundary elements to representing shade, actual texture, and surface. The idea of lines blending beyond the boundary was also a trait of the Impressionist art Dow

42 *Early Beginnings*

was familiar with, especially from his travels to Europe. Many, including John La Farge, were interested in blurring the blots of paint rather than drawing discrete lines to draw outlines of forms.

Differently, Denman Ross's work displayed more of an interest in the intellectual apparatus. It is possible that because Ross was mostly drawing, coloring shapes, or taking photographs for the purposes of his design theory, materials may not have been binding his process as much, or was influencing it in different ways. The evidence for Ross's interest on how materials changed the visual quality of a work exists in his collection of pixilated photographs printed in magazines and newspapers. Ross magnified some of these to accentuate the pixilated quality of the print. Different from the abstract line grids Ross superimposed on images, this image was a grid of dots of different densities. A field of dots was also consistent with the arrangement of elements in *A Theory of Pure Design*. The magnified prints and the display of diffusing boundary lines resemble the pointillist approach to painting at the time (Figure 2.1). Ross seems to have been interested in observing a new kind of organizational structure in the image and in how line was no longer the only boundary-defining element.

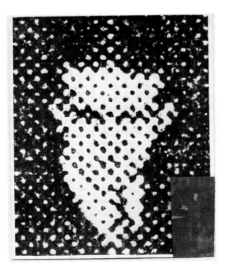

Figure 2.1 Pixellated image of young man with photograph inset, undated.

Source: Denman Waldo Ross Study Materials, box 31. Harvard Art Museums Archives, Harvard University, Cambridge, MA.

Abstract Forms and Form Relations: Dow   43

While Ross allowed his students to experiment with form, Dow emphasized techniques. Evidently, Ross's formal experimentation used what we can call the intellectual apparatus. The triangles in the photography analyses, or the grid underlying the wallpaper designs, exemplify such attempts. Still, Ross was not engaged in a design process unless he considered the analyses to be abstract compositions. He most obviously showed his intention to engage in an active role when he tried to make changes in the photographs. Dow's guidelines, framing and notan were also intellectual tools. Overall, both Ross and Dow acquired an abstraction, which seems to be the key point to these analyses. It is interwoven with various aspects of their work, such as the techniques they chose to use, the influences of European Impressionists and Post-impressionists along with photography, natural sciences and the Orient. The abstraction they acquired was not a timeless approach but a synthetic one, as Dow announced in the title page of his *Composition*, and it was to serve a pedagogical purpose. Ross and Dow's treatises allude to their understanding of dynamics in the design process but mainly outline fundamentals of design for teaching. These principles, when viewed in isolation, are often not much more than what other theories and formalisms have offered throughout history. Their significant viewpoint on design teaching, regarding the personal development of the student, mainly comes to light through marginal aspects of their work discernible in their public lectures on education, exercises they give to students, and their personal notes and analyses.

Bibliography

Adams, Henry. "The Mind of John La Farge." In *John La Farge: [Exhibition]: Carnegie Museum of Art, Pittsburgh; National Museum of American Art, Smithsonian Institution, Washington, D.C.* New York: Abbeville Press, Inc., 1987, pp. 11–77.

Dow, Arthur Wesley. Arthur Wesley Dow papers. Archives of American Art/ Smithsonian Institution. [Microfilm reels 1208–1209, 1271, 1079, 3620, 1027, 1033–1034].

Dow, Arthur Wesley. *Composition: A Series of Exercises in Art Structure for the Use of Students and Teachers.* Berkeley, CA: University of California Press, 1997 [1899, 1920].

Dow, Arthur Wesley. Sixth and last lecture in the course titled "~~Modern~~ Landscape Painting" given to the Board of Education, November 8, 1905. Arthur W. Dow Collection, Ipswich Historical Society Archive, Ipswich, MA.

44 Early Beginnings

Dow, Arthur Wesley. Draft for a talk given at Kindergarten Association in Philadelphia, February 15, 1906. Arthur W. Dow Collection, Ipswich Historical Society Archive, Ipswich, MA.

Dow, Arthur Wesley. "Talks on Appreciation of Art, No. I." *The Delineator* (January 1915): 15.

Dow, Arthur Wesley. "Talks on Appreciation of Art, No. IV, Color." *The Delineator* (February 1916): 15.

Dow, Arthur Wesley. An Explanation of Certain Methods of Art Teaching: Q & A. Arthur W. Dow Collection, Ipswich Historical Society Archive, Ipswich, MA.

Frank, Marie. "The Theory of Pure Design and American Architectural Education in the Early Twentieth Century." *Journal of the Society of Architectural Historians*, v. 67, n. 2 (June 2008), 248–273.

Green, Nancy and Jessie Poesch. *Arthur Wesley Dow and American Arts & Crafts*. New York: The American Federation of Arts, 1999.

La Farge, John. *The Higher Life in Art*. New York: The McClure Company, 1908.

Moffat, Frederick C. *Arthur Wesley Dow (1857–1922)*. Washington, DC: The Smithsonian Institution Press, 1977.

3 The Psychology for Basic Design in the Late Nineteenth Century

Character development is, undoubtedly, an ambitious objective for any educational program. Nevertheless, this is precisely what Türel Saranli, a Turkish design educator, associates with basic design education (1998, 39). A century earlier, in the introductory chapter to *Composition*, Arthur W. Dow states that learning design, as a preparation to drawing in his case, is basically "training the judgment" (1997 [1899, 1920], 64). Both approaches entail what educational sciences refer to as attitudes, a type of competence complementary to knowledge and skills in education. Attitudes are not necessarily as burdensome to the instructor and the student as character development first sounds and many art and design schools today involve the core of what is known as basic design education in their curricula as the individual development of the student as designer. It is also common, however, to bring knowledge and skills to the forefront in curriculum designs as these competences are seemingly easier to assess, whereas attitudes are left to tacit learning as issues of taboo. In a different manner, in the basic design approaches presented in this book, attitudes cannot be detached from knowledge and skills.

Historically, basic design education as individual development can be traced back to the early nineteenth-century child educators, Johann H. Pestalozzi and Friedrich Froebel, and their pedagogies of hands-on learning (Naylor, 1985, 77). Revolutionary theories of hands-on learning, or learning by doing, in child education involved physically acting situations out, using hands and body during play in guided ways and playing with toys that are suitable for flexible engagement, such as building blocks. The craft-oriented and rationalized learning advocated

46 *Early Beginnings*

by Denman W. Ross and Arthur W. Dow continued the controlled but playful engagement with matter. The intellectual context of their time, partly based on the developments in the field of psychology in relation to the arts, sensations, and education had an effect on their approach. Ross and Dow introduced tools to abstract, and therefore manage dynamic part–whole relations in the visual field and the experience-based material world of art and design. These tools served a learner-centered pedagogical agenda to foster unique designers and thinkers.

An additional backdrop to Ross and Dow's educational approaches was in the art and design education scene prior to their time. The State of Massachusetts legislature had passed an Act in 1870 to mandate the teaching of "industrial and mechanical" drawing as required courses in public schools (Singerman, 1999, 13). This was a testament to democratize society through enabling individuals both intellectually and as a workforce by providing fundamental aptitudes. From this Act onwards, there was an increase in the numbers of university-trained art teachers and in drawing/art/crafts courses taught in elementary and secondary schools. With an understanding of the good that the liberal arts can bring to undergraduate education, the overall belief was that knowledge unifies the individual and culture (ibid., 14). Singerman (ibid.) as well as Stankiewicz *et al.* (2004) provide detailed accounts of the developing university-level education of arts in that period.

Ross understood that students acquire personal values through experience in physical tasks usually geared towards developing technical ability. In his public address at the Rhode Island School of Design in 1903, Ross observed that, in hands-on learning, the student "thinks in the materials, in the terms, in the forms of effort and exertion belonging to the art in which his work has to be done" (1903, 10). So personal engagement with materials in consciously operated processes is crucial. Design thinking is interlinked with the actions of the body with regards to the physical world. The materials and the relevant techniques to process these materials have a direct impact on thought processes in design.

Against the timeless and universal principles imposed on aesthetic phenomena, personal development cultivates one's own principles in relating to a world that is perceived in changing ways. Sensory experiences play into the development of the individual thinker. One way in

The Psychology for Basic Design 47

which Ross and Dow's abstract forms facilitate the utility of the senses in the design process is through the simplicity of forms and form relations they idolize in their methods. The painter and critic Roger Fry recognized that "the disturbance of purely decorative values by reason of the representative effect takes place, and the problem becomes too complex for geometrical proof" (Fry, 1920, 21). The eye is able to focus on singular relationships in abstract or simple or "meaningless" forms. At the same time, the unfamiliarity caused by the lack of meaning requires a fresh eye in experience. Accordingly, relations between forms change with the experience. Neither can forms be conceived as ideal in any way, nor the relations between them as fixed principles. Abstract forms and their relations that are open to interpretation facilitate these exploratory situations.

The notion of sensations as recognized in nineteenth-century psychological and philosophical works provides a backdrop to Ross and Dow's practice of abstract forms and form relations. The eighteenth-century empiricism and psychophysiological research in Germany on the connection of the mind and the body culminate in the philosophical work of American Pragmatist William James. James's idea of sagacity is traceable in Ross and Dow's approach as well as in other movements in art to which the two educators were exposed. Also comparable to Ross and Dow's understanding of changing part–whole relations in perception and thought, are the dynamic worldviews that were developing at the time. The organicist position in art and architecture links to then-recent scientific assessments regarding the growth of life. Simultaneously, descriptions of the universe incorporated the notion of process and changing part–whole relations. These epistemological connections set the stage for basic design education.

3.1 Senses and Perceptiveness

Integrating senses into the design process contributes to the (empiricist) stipulation that creative knowledge is not all innate or learnt, but also provisionally developed through experience. For example, hands-on experimentation with materials allows the individual to see in materials qualities that are beyond what is conventionally known. There are numerous examples of this in the tradition of basic design education. One

48　*Early Beginnings*

is the common exercise in folding, which focuses on discovering how flimsy materials like paper can be (made) sturdy. Such an exercise aims to take a well-known material outside of its common functionality, or to work with materials not yet known in application, and try new treatments and usage. Another example, from the Bauhaus, is testing the tensile and compression limits of paper as a variety of techniques, such as sewing and pinning rather than gluing, are tried to fasten pieces of it. Josef Albers describes how the purpose of these explorations is not to "always create 'works of art'" but rather "gathering 'experience'" (cited in Wingler, 1969, 42).

What these exercises demonstrate is perhaps an act of *revealing* some unforeseen qualities as in a phenomenological approach, but it is not assumed here that there is a finitely described universe being disclosed for one to discover at a time. There is not one Truth, waiting to unfold. Instead, students try new definitions and ascribe new perceptions to materials to explore many possibilities indefinitely. From each combination of materials and actions a new experience emerges, not just another combination. A finite description of the universe implies that all parts are fixed. Definitions are rather created when necessary, and the universe can be defined in indefinitely many ways. Presumptive existence of concepts, however complex and detailed, inhibits further exploration of the senses in changing contexts. The purpose of the exercises, we deduce from Albers, is to change the context for either the known materials or the known processes in order to allow for new perceptions of each. Limitations in creative processes will come momentarily as part of the material, technical, and psychological circumstances involved. Designers will also be able to assign limitations according to desired strategies. Assuming them upfront is unnecessary.

Early nineteenth-century research in psychophysiology by German psychologists such as Johannes Müller, Hermann von Helmholtz, and Wilhelm Wundt shaped the late nineteenth-century development of modern psychology in America (Boring, 1950 [1929]). We also see the influences of eighteenth-century British empiricism in the philosophy of the time. That idea that principles are not innate but come from experience (Locke, 1993 [1689]) and that vision is prior to form (Berkeley, 1709) prepare the way for American Pragmatists, who distance themselves

The Psychology for Basic Design 49

from the Cartesian division between the mind and the body. William James recognized the external world and the subjective inner experience as a continuum and wrote that consciousness, from birth onwards, "is of a teeming multiplicity of objects and relations" and isolated sensations can only be "the results of discriminative attention" (James, 1983 [1890], 219).

Contextual apprehension and discriminatory attention directly link to what James calls "sagacity" (as an indispensable part of reasoning) in *Principles of Psychology* (1983 [1890], 957). He inherits this term from John Locke, who explains that, in intuitive logic, sagacity is the ability to apply "intermediate ideas" to discover "the agreement or disagreement of any other" (Locke, 1993 [1689], 297) Stiny (2006) matches sagacity to plain and contemporary terms as the concept of embedding, a part relation between two shapes of similar elements (e.g. shapes that are made up of only lines) where "one shape is part of another shape whenever every maximal element of the first is embedded in a maximal element of the second" (ibid., 184). Our eyes constantly do this: visually, we are able to embed shapes in other shapes, e.g. my 5-year-old daughter cuts out any shape she wants from a blank sheet of paper. What Locke calls sagacity, J. S. Mill calls good observing, and James refers to it elsewhere as mode of conceiving. In the wallpaper patterns by Denman W. Ross, varying modes of conceiving allowed for different combinations of units. Different parts of units were taken into consideration for each new relation. At the same time, newly perceived parts led to non-combinatorial designs. The final motif designs were not necessarily the sum of their parts but more. The simple example on the left side of Figure 3.1 is from one of

Figure 3.1 Details from Ross *et al.* (1900), Plates 10 and 12.
Note: Emphases by the author.
Source: Ross *et al.* (1900).

50   *Early Beginnings*

Ross's wallpaper pattern exercises and it illustrates how two of the given units are applied in the design. A shape that is picked out from one of these units, and a shape that two back-to-back copies of the other are embedded in, form two new parts for the design. The smaller one is distinctively not a combination of given parts, but a newly perceived part in a given part.

Sagacity explains the visual ability to pick out parts within wholes where and when they are relevant. It implies a selection process based on perception partial to context, allowing for all kinds of individual biases, conscious or not. Moreover, wholes can be perceived differently as Gestalt switches occur as in the example shown above for individual shapes. Ross's cut in the four-pods shape reflects how he defines its features. And at another time, the same unit shape may be defined differently and cut differently by Ross or someone else. To the right of Figure 3.1, we can see the small unit from the wallpaper pattern on the left is applied differently. In this case, Ross's student, Edgar O. Parker applies his own visual rule and cuts the unit shape differently. This cut is in direct relation to how he will use this shape in his designs. He cuts out two of the bulging sides in accordance with where he will place it in the design. In an alternate scenario, he could have produced this new small shape by joining two circles that are also a part of the given vocabulary. These decisions may seem trivial at first but constitute important small steps in one's training to make judgments and consciously manipulate form relations, which in turn will reflect on the making of design decisions with broader impact beyond forms.

Ross's analyses of photography provides another example. The tool of abstraction that Ross introduces in his analyses facilitates the definition and picking out of parts. Ross uses these abstract guidelines to refer to parts of the image and their relations as he sees them. His students are expected, in turn, to use different lines and systems of lines to see parts they were traditionally not trained to.

3.2 Dynamic Worldviews

The broader philosophical context to the particular capacity of the individual in constructing unique worldviews directly or indirectly had an effect on the development of a critical perspective in scientific

The Psychology for Basic Design 51

methodology at the turn of twentieth century. The critical perspective in scientific thought then was, first, at a level that addressed the problems of industrialism and the practical implications of scientific progress. The Arts and Crafts Movement resonated with this level. At another level, there was the philosophical problem of how we perceive a world with ever-changing definitions. The critique formed mainly to challenge the confidence in establishing timeless concepts in science. *A priori* and timeless definitions disregard the perceptual context that is constantly changing. William James often indicated wariness towards the conventional reductionist approach to vision and fixed mental processes in German psychology. James acknowledged that humans rely on conceptual decompositions of the life they live and experience all the time. Yet he also recognized the insufficiency of intellect in performing tasks that are so naturally carried out by sense-experience (1996 [1908], 256). Questioning the static and constrained view of intellectualism, he praised the dynamic plurality of intuitions. Finding that clarity in definitions is pretentious at best, James observed that definitions could not incessantly match the ever-changing perceptions and experiences.

Pragmatist thought was a part of the spirit of the time in the Western world. Temporal aspects of experience challenged static notions of space and systems of thought across various scientific disciplines and a general dynamic worldview formed in science and philosophy. In physics, philosophy and biology, concepts of temporal change and changing relations played a part in new theories. The theories of the anatomist Georges Cuvier (1769–1832) on organic wholes, and Sir Charles Lyell (1797–1875) on geological development over time led to Herbert Spencer's treatises on synthetic philosophy, which included sociology, biology, and psychology (1855–1898), evolution (1887), as well as to Charles Darwin's discourse on species and selection (1859–1871). These works contributed to the views on dynamic systems in physics and philosophy in nineteenth-century America. Philosopher Philip P. Wiener (1972 [1949]) explores the connection to Pragmatist thought in detail in his book, *Evolution and the Founders of Pragmatism*. The relational view and process philosophy of Alfred North Whitehead (1920), another renowned American Pragmatist followed and expanded the connection of Pragmatism to a dynamic worldview.

52   *Early Beginnings*

Although the intellectual climate provides a context, the work of James and other Pragmatists overall contributes a viewpoint that digresses from this historical and epistemological continuance. Richard Hofstadter points this out in comparison with the position held by Herbert Spencer that the environment is "a fixed norm" to observe and generalize a theory of evolutionary system, whereas "Pragmatism, entertaining a more positive view of the activities of the organism, looked upon the environment as something that could be manipulated" (Hofstadter, 1962 [1944]), 123–124).

The notion of continuity between the subject and the object in the Pragmatist view gives rise to an understanding of the universe as an ongoing process which holds potential for change from within. This is a perspective that resonates with the philosophies of design that Ross and Dow, as unspoken pragmatists, implicitly developed and practiced. Their world was of course the world of design, the space of forms and materials, and the designer.

In parallel to Hofstadter's account with regards to the disconnect between pragmatists and evolution theory, Pragmatism as a philosophy of design is incoherent with the usually cited organicism in designs of the period. As art historian Caroline van Eck (1994, 20) observes, organicism in nineteenth-century art and architecture is usually interpreted in terms of the idea of organic unity where parts have a functional correlation to each other and the whole. This is more in line with the instrumentalism in Cuvier's anatomical or Darwin's biological findings, where parts are distinct and follow a formal idealism imposed by the whole they belong to. The organicist view which Kevin Nute (1997) attributes to Arthur Dow and Ernest Fenollosa, Dow's mentor in ideas of the organic, is not very different. This organicist view focuses on "organic wholeness" as "mutual interdependence of each contributing part." Fenollosa's writing from 1891 brings the notion of a fixed whole to the forefront:

A true synthetic whole cannot have a single part added or subtracted without destroying the peculiar character of its wholeness, without disturbing the perfect equilibrium of the mutual modifications. Thus such a synthetic whole is an individual, a separate

The Psychology for Basic Design   53

entity, [with] a peculiar organic nature, an unchangeable possibility, a foreordained unit from all eternity.

(cited in Nute, 1997, 273)

Fenollosa's knowledge of organic systems and their dynamics is not obvious, but Nute points out that Fenollosa was interested in Nature, even as demonstrated in Japanese art, as a source of unique, ideal beauty in line with the idealist Western take on aesthetics at the time. Nute associates this interest with

a combination of the Kantian concept of the purely formal 'aesthetic idea' exemplified by the organic whole, and Hegel's metaphysical explanation of the unique appeal of the organic form as the most complete material manifestation of the Spirit or metaphysical 'Idea'

and concludes that for Fenollosa, Japanese art was not representative of a different type of organicism but only the means "to teach about the nature of art in general" (ibid., 273).

Ross and Dow both knew and worked with Ernest Fenollosa personally. They also had interest in natural forms as well as in Japanese art. Ross collected scientific images, and drawn analyses of organic forms and body systems (such as skeletons), showing various rhythmic structures found in nature. Figure 3.2 shows images that Ross collected to attest to this interest. They are "fragments of leaves partially eaten by insects ..." as the original figure captions identify. Ross was interested in the variance of rhythmic patterns as well as variance within the patterns.

While Ross drew attention to the variety between species with different anatomies and life patterns, Dow observed nature in a painterly way. Among his notes in the Arthur Wesley Dow papers, in the Archives of American Art/Smithsonian Institution are neatly drawn figures of "barberry" and "tirillium" petals with a caption that reads "design." Both sketches are carefully constructed as symmetric shapes. He presumed and directly used rules of axial and rotational symmetry, along with scale transformations to create side by side two formal variations of flowers. As this documentation shows, Dow was interested in understanding aesthetic organization in nature and how he could reconstruct it on paper.

54 *Early Beginnings*

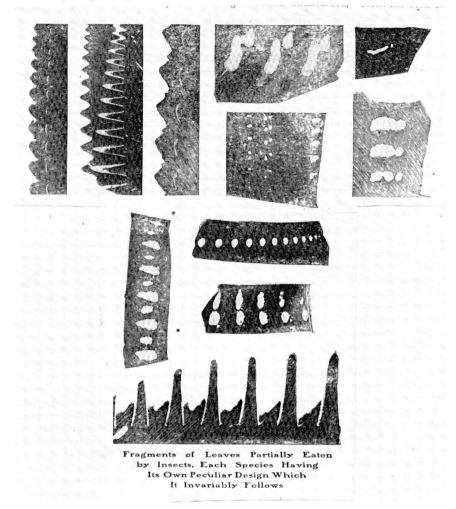

Figure 3.2 Clipping of "Fragments of Leaves Partially Eaten by Insects…", undated.
Source: Denman Waldo Ross Study Materials, box 29. Harvard Art Museums Archives, Harvard University, Cambridge, MA.

Yet, for art and design, there is more to be gained from organic systems if one looks beyond static hierarchies of interdependent parts. An alternative history of organic theories in art and design would have to include pragmatists, both the philosophers and the artists, two of whom are Ross and Dow as they recognize dynamic relations in organic

The Psychology for Basic Design 55

systems and pursue control of them. Dow's flower sketches may indicate a conventional interest in symmetries of natural form. Nevertheless, admiring a flower for its static order of beauty changes its color when one sees it as a design that can be reconstructed by certain tools and altered form relations. Dow generally employs this latter perspective in his diagrams. His nature photography provides more evidence. Spatial relations that he captures simply reflect his direct experiences in nature and not so much the deductive, mathematical, and scientific formula. Furthermore, as Nancy E. Green and Jessie Poesch (1999, 76) acknowledge, Dow used photography as part of a design methodology too. Dow's photography were studies for his landscape paintings. Similar to the prints that bring about the contrasts of light and dark tonalities, Dow's photography served as experiments of notan. Green and Poesch (ibid., 76) propose that Dow also might have manipulated and printed variations from the negatives of the photographs.

In addition to the potential with light and shade, Dow used his theories of design and composition in his photography. Recognizing that the framing of a photograph is a design problem, he was interested in manipulating the image just as he would do with compositional drawing or painting. A photograph he took in 1912 entitled "Pacific Grove" shows how he frames the scene in the same way that he frames his landscape paintings (ibid., 92). Dow framed landscape in photography in the ways he would for paintings. The structural forms were not in nature but were what he created to picture it. They were temporary tools.

What Dow wrote in *Composition* regarding abstract landscape exercises applies to the said photograph as well: "Looking out from a grove we notice that trees, vertical and straight lines, cut horizontal lines – an arrangement in Opposition and Repetition making a pattern in rectangular spaces" (1997 [1899, 1920], 104). The underlying organization of this particular composition in photography could easily have been the lines shown in the analysis. Dow used his usual framework of vertical and horizontal lines as his tools in framing the landscape and creates a unique way of observing it.

Like Fenollosa, or many others at that time, Dow might have been wanting to capture the unique ideal beauty. But the fact that we have access to his tools of abstraction, and that these, as well those of Ross,

56 *Early Beginnings*

were subject to change according to persons and times, shows that Dow and Ross were more interested in unique experiences of nature than in capturing an ideal. In their pedagogical approaches, they were trying to encourage students to experience what is around them sagaciously with tools of abstraction that they would create. Unlike the typical interpretations of organicism in the art and design of the time, the notion of parts and wholes did not necessarily imply set hierarchical relations that the trained eye would recognize in nature. These hierarchies were only a possible definition. Especially in spatial or visual experiences, parts were not always distinct to begin with. Every part that was identified as a part at one particular time could have been identified as a whole at another time.

In the context of design teaching with a focus on process, this is even more crucial to observe than ever. This idea had already been partially adopted, whether or not as a direct result of the developments in psychology of vision, in the nineteenth-century child education that preceded Dow and Ross. Friedrich Froebel's agenda in child education was to encourage looking for "parts of wholes," in order to understand more about the universe (2001c [1899, 1902]). Froebel created his educational tools called gifts (mock-ups of the external world) and occupations (strategies from the inner world), based on four main groups of wholes, and showed how each could be a part in the other. He was following geometric truisms in defining a framework: points, lines, planes, and solids. This vocabulary was very much similar to what Wassily Kandinsky of the Bauhaus proposed years later in his theories of form. The categories of various objects in the gifts all served a purpose. Just as with the elements of Pure Design, beads (points) could be used to make a necklace (a curved line) and "thread (line) could be woven into fabric (plane), or be wrapped in a yarn (solid)" (Froebel, 2001a [1888]).

Although there were similarities in defining elements to be used in the construction of various forms, Ross's Pure Design was a step ahead. The number of relations between parts in the framework Froebel proposes was limited. The dynamic arrangements in the wallpaper patterns were significantly different. Ross's multifaceted units came together in various spatial relations. As explained earlier, this is partial, concerning how parts were perceived at each moment. Still, similarities existed between

The Psychology for Basic Design 57

the approaches. In Froebel's gift sets, part–whole dynamics were actually explored in the child's interaction with the gifts. The interaction, which Froebel called occupations, included molding, carving, weaving, cutting, folding, etc. Through these, the child engaged in forming new relations between the units. Later, Arthur Dow listed similar craft activities as part of a creative education program: leather, metal and wood carving, modeling in clay, wax, plaster, and papier mâché, printing, batik, textiles, paper, etc. The engagement with materials was crucial for the individual to recognize the factors that guided the interaction in creating a form. Both Froebel and Dow set an unknown precedence to the Bauhaus model where all the different crafts were central to the foundation curriculum.

The notion of part–whole relations extended to another level in Froebel's pedagogy. Froebel explained that his pedagogy aims to develop a feeling of personality in the child. This, according to Froebel, was the means to perception, and happens when "the child feels itself a part-whole" (2001c [1899, 1902]). Gifts and occupations allow the child to connect to the world as a unique, active and changing part in it. Johannes Itten, who set up the basic design course at the Weimar Bauhaus two decades later, applied this continuous relation between mind and external matter in his pedagogy. Due to his background in Froebelian kindergarten teaching, he stressed the unique qualities of the individual, self-expression and self-discovery as the guides for individual students on their own individual paths. He described his pedagogical approach based on students' intuition with fervor: "In teaching the means of design it seemed important to me to appeal to diverse individual temperaments and talents ... First, imagination and creative ability must be freed and strengthened" (Itten, 1963, 7–8).

In terms of personal development, Itten's view followed the general motivation behind basic design education. However, there is a more contemporary way to elaborate on the means to design and discuss whether "intuitive finding" in design pedagogy can be reinterpreted as the utility of senses as a key factor in the self-conscious thought process.

3.3 Senses and Perceptiveness in Art and Design

Utility of senses was tried in the context of basic design education as early as nineteenth century. Ross and Dow's work is exemplary. But basic

58 *Early Beginnings*

design education history, mostly the legacy of the Bauhaus, usually points to other links in psychology, such as the theories of empathy and Gestalt. These theories are based on sense perception but do not explore the senses as active parts of reasoning. For example, Rudolf Arnheim (1969, 29), a prominent twentieth-century Gestalt psychologist, accepts that there would be a preregistered order to an image and that the perceiver would see that. He writes, "The perception of the shape is the grasping of generic structural features (found in, or imposed upon, the stimulus material)." He illustrates this in his example of a square that is divided into four equal parts. The sides of the square are its "genuine parts – that is, sections representing a segregated subwhole within the total context" (Arnheim, 1974 [1954], 78). Arnheim continues that a swastika is "obviously" not a part of this square divided into four "because the local connections and segregations that form the swastika are overruled by others in the context of the square" (ibid., 77–78). Arnheim supposes that the definition of the square, thus the context it sets for looking at it, are fixed. Visually, it is not so. Seeing other shapes in the square is possible in other contexts and so is reasoning.

Arnheim also uses the expression "mere portions or pieces" referring to "sections segregated only in relation to a limited local context or to no inherent breaks in the figure at all" (ibid., 78). The equilateral cross with four bent legs would be an example of this as well. Arnheim continues to claim that these are "mistakes" and "misinterpretations" (ibid., 77). In his Gestaltist viewpoint, the whole and its parts always seem to be fixed. In a creative process, however, the surprising portions and pieces that are visible in local contexts are more interesting than the "genuine" parts (ibid., 78).

Arnheim follows a tradition that was established by Kurt Koffka and Max Wortheimer who developed the Gestalt theory in late nineteenth and early twentieth centuries. Nevertheless the notions of Gestalt perception had arisen earlier, in the psychological works of Wilhelm Wundt and were implied in some of the late nineteenth-century art works. For instance, in 1908, painter John La Farge gave visual examples of Gestalt, and switches between black forms and white background. Significantly different from Arnheim, La Farge talks of a switch between Gestalts as a conscious act of selection that is welcome in the artistic process, too:

The Psychology for Basic Design   59

If the [certain lines] are very important to us, we see none but those, and not the ones that cross them, however distinctly these may all be traced. That is to say, that voluntarily and by effort we strengthen the sensation we wish to have, and weaken the one that we do not care for ... Thus if on a white surface I trace two concentric circles, I can look upon the image as representing two black rings, and I shall see black rings; or I can look at the interval between the circles, and see a white ring ...

(1908, 100–101)

Few of Dow's ideas are also precursors to the Gestalt approach. For example, Dow's notan exercises are merely illustrations of figure–ground relations. Moreover, Dow used the concept as a pedagogical system of abstraction. In his *Talks on Appreciation of Art*, Dow instructed how to abstract pictures – such as by Corot – in black and white spots:

Put a piece of tissue paper over one of the pictures, and with a soft pencil blacken all the dark shapes. You will produce flat tones like [directs to a figure] ... There is a big leading spot or mass – of light or of dark – and all the others are grouped with it and seem to belong to it as if they were all in one family. Your tracing will show you this [directs to a figure]. Or, turn the picture upside down and you will readily see what I mean.

(1915b, 15)

This process is similar in its effectiveness to drawing vertical and horizontal lines to simplify an image to understand simpler form relations. Dow selectively perceived wholes, or sometimes parts. He was interested not in the fact that dark forms gather together on a white background, but more in understanding and conveying the simple relation between dark and light. Just as perpendicular lines are abstractions of landscapes, dark and light together form an abstraction of a colorful picture.

Examples of Gestalt perception in literature on the subject usually show switches between two different perceptions as in black and white figure–ground, or filling in the blanks in point or line drawings to reveal a whole shape that is already known. Actual Gestalt possibilities exceed

60   *Early Beginnings*

these binary relations. Similar to Ross's perceptual changes in pattern designs, being open to all possible perceptions is important. Ross and Dow's application of perceptual switches differs from the idea of a preconceived Gestalt. Seeing with a fresh eye each time is part of what makes each design process unique and creative. Sketching is often praised as the tool of design thinking. Its benefit is along the same lines. An idea is put down on paper and another is taken from it. A pragmatist would recognize the changing perception of shapes with infinitely many possibilities to offer. James, for instance, gave multiple descriptions to a shape, and implied that there might be many more. With reference to a star of David, he wrote:

> We conceive a given reality in this way or in that, to suit our purpose, and the reality passively submits to the conception ... You can treat the adjoined figures as a star, as two big triangles crossing each other, as a hexagon with legs set up on its angles, as six triangles hanging together by their tips, etc. ... No one of them is false. Which may be treated as the more true, depends altogether on the human use of it.
>
> (James, 1995 [1907], 97)

The Bauhaus methodology is known to have followed Gestalt psychology especially in the later years of the School. Nevertheless, for Itten, one of the very first instructors at the Bauhaus, the pedagogical methods for creating personal experience in the students resonated with another psychological notion: empathy. Empathy was first elaborated as a psychological theory of art around 1870 by Robert Vischer, and was developed by psychologist Theodore Lipps around 1900. The term is also traced to late nineteenth-century German texts on aesthetics, perception and space (Mallgrave, 1994). Empathy is the unconditional connection between formal properties of an object and sense apparatus (from muscles to emotions). Lipps' contemporary, art historian Wilhelm Worringer wrote that empathy reflects a confidence in the world as it is (Worringer, 1997 [1953]). Evidently, the Bauhaus instructor Johannes Itten's interest in the connection of the self to the external world referred to empathy. Gillian Naylor (1985, 77) describes how, in the drawing

The Psychology for Basic Design 61

course, Itten had his students cry before an image of Magdalene, and roar before that of a tiger in preparation for drawing either image. This was a way for the student to develop one's own grasp of a phenomenon in an interpretative imitation of nature. However, that a tiger roars and Magdalene cries are biases that guide that imitation, and the act is contradictory to the interpretative aim.

Dow's approach was reactionary to imitating nature altogether. This is despite the fact that he painted numerous landscapes. He was concerned that sense perceptions were reduced to symbols in imitations of nature, as well as painting from memory. He referred to these as "picture-writing" (Dow, January 1915a) and was against the long tradition of "teaching art through imitation" of styles and nature. This tradition undermined the artist's comprehension of the structure. About copying form nature, he wrote: "so much modern painting is but picture-writing; only story-telling, not art; and so much architecture and decoration only dead copies of conventional motive" (Dow, 1997 [1899, 1920], 64).

The theory of empathy focuses more on the connection between the object and the observer, rather than the artist/designer. In contrast to empathy, Worringer describes another type of volition, namely, abstraction, where man reacts to uncertainties, and transcends them into absolutes: "the urge to abstraction is the outcome of a great inner unrest inspired in man by the phenomena of the outside world" (Worringer, 1997 [1953], 15). His directions for how to abstract through taking

> the object of the external world out of its natural context, out of the unending flux of being, to purify it of all its dependence upon life, i.e. of everything about it that was arbitrary, to render it necessary and irrefragable

culminate in an approximation of the object to "its *absolute* value" (ibid., 17).

Deliberating on uncertainties is part of the basic design education agenda, but the objective is not to turn them into timeless certainties. Differently, abstraction, as illustrated in Ross and Dow's work, starts from a feeling of unrest, and sustains it. Ross and Dow's pedagogies

62   *Early Beginnings*

showed how to set up temporary frameworks, instead of submitting to any predetermined structures. Frameworks then were open to further development based on variance in sense perception.

Art history has generally put emphasis on the influence of the German psychological tradition on early twentieth-century avant-garde design education in Europe. The common account brings America into the picture only after these avant-gardes fled the Continent prior to and during the Second World War. Then again, William James, who was the contemporary of Ross and Dow, was already taking a leading part in the same psychological tradition as early as the late nineteenth century. James's background was in experimental psychology as developed by Wilhelm Wundt and Hermann von Helmholtz, that led to empathy and Gestalt theories. His point of view, however, was different, maybe characteristic of philosophical schools only in America at the time. William J. Gavin summarizes the assumptions in psychology James reacted against: "We accept experience as finished; we assume experience is made of substantive parts; we rely too much on language, which is exclusive" (Gavin, 1992, 18).

James acknowledges the "ambiguity" and "indeterminateness" of visual perception (1983, 864–869). In contrast, symbolisms like language "abridge thought and fix terms" (ibid., 933). But indeterminateness is not only a trait of the visual sense. It is common to all experience and James applies its properties to consciousness (thought) at large. Every thought is personal, ever changing, continuous, independent of the object that it deals with, and is based on a selection of parts of the object it deals with (ibid., 220).

The psychological tradition that was influential in art is mostly thought to have served for the scientific validation of art. Regarding how Pragmatism relates to art, the opposite seems to be true. James's ideas on indeterminateness in thought and perception probably formed during his formal training in painting where he was able to grasp "the evanescent moment of experience" (Matthiessen, cited in Adams 1985, 65). James shared the influence of ideas with John La Farge, a painter and an art theorist knowledgeable in contemporary science. James and La Farge met in William Morris Hunt's painting classes as early as 1859. With respect to visual uncertainties, techniques such as blurring outlines of figures, pointillist application of paint, and abstraction were developing features in nineteenth-century painting. La Farge also practiced these techniques. His interpretation of Leonardo's teaching "to look for help in composition to the spottings and veinings of marble, the breaks and disintegration of old walls" may have prompted the blurred images in his paintings (La Farge, 1908, 98).

John La Farge painted in the Impressionistic style and experimented with the idea of blurring the image, as in examples of his work such as *Flowers on a window ledge* (oil on canvas) from 1861. He explored the potential of paint and brush rather than trying to make sharp outlines. Henry Adams describes the blurry potential of La Farge's work:

> Rather than presenting the image as fixed in a sharp focus that does not vary with distance and light, as was customary in American painting at this time, La Farge presents optical vibrations, a sea of different luminosities, colorations, and degrees of focus.
>
> (1985, 60)

Blurred images allowed these accidents of vision. Pointillist style was briefly mentioned earlier with reference to Ross's interest in pixilated photographs. Although Ross's intent was not clear, the photographs, presumably blown up by Ross, illustrated the blurring of boundaries and how points, as elements of design, came together to create a whole. Once again using a tool of abstraction or an analysis, Ross might have been exploring the varying visions of design.

The paths of Dow and Ross constantly crossed with Pragmatist philosophers, such as William James, George Santayana, and John Dewey, who all wrote extensively on art in its relation to experience. Ross personally knew James, and his design theory course in the Architecture and Fine Arts Department at Harvard University (1899–1935) coincided with James's professorship in psychology and philosophy there between 1880 and 1907. Also, in multiple letters, there is evidence that students simultaneously took classes from Ross and James, and his colleague George Santayana, who also taught at Harvard between 1899 and 1912 and wrote on aesthetics. The same applied to Dow in relation to Dewey. He taught at Teachers College in Columbia University from

64 *Early Beginnings*

1908 to 1922 and took part in John Dewey's efforts there to establish active learning in education (1905–1930).

Nevertheless, neither Ross nor Dow explicitly wrote about uncertainties, perhaps because it was a little radical, especially for Ross, who chose to see design as a science even if science for him was more a means than an end. In basic design pedagogy, vagueness permeates aspects of the design process other than just the visual. For example, vagueness is encouraged when a problem is given. Little explanation follows, so that students are able to develop their own ideas about what it might be. It is a push towards creating one's own thinking. Another example of vagueness is found at the end of an assignment. Evaluation is not based on general rules. Rather, there is a different critique for almost every object produced; the reasoning behind it is discussed; its form is open for debate; evaluation is done openly in a group, where projects are selected not for better–worse value but for their discussion value. Every individual is expected to see for their own self and not through anybody else's eyes. Seeing through others' eyes might work in other cases such as in the sciences where a systematic build-up of knowledge is required. But in education for creative thinking, seeing for yourself is especially essential because it is how you select an object, and set up a relation in a unique way.

In addition to their association with trends in nineteenth-century painting, Ross and Dow's involvement in arts and crafts links the discussion of vagueness to their design teaching methods. As was the case with John La Farge, who formed his ideas on the creative process from his involvement with stained glass, their interest in arts and crafts created a direct relation with the material context. Decorative arts were a stepping-stone for content-free form studies, where a modern understanding of abstraction prevented it from being turned into a formal code. Instead of following methods for learning accepted in the guild system, such as copying the master for technique (empathy), Ross and Dow used material and technique to create frameworks that would help flex conceptual definitions. For example, Ross's busy but abstract forms in wallpaper patterns stimulate different reactions and constitute a formal design exercise where abstract ornament helps the student focus on form relations and becomes the tool to think with in other contexts. Ross and

The Psychology for Basic Design 65

Dow present abstraction as a tool to think about form relations intuitively. Their systems of abstraction, allowing for the plurality that is necessary for creativity, tame uncertainties of perception only momentarily and in the context of the "evanescent moments of experience" (Matthiesen, cited in Adams 1985, 65).

Diverging from the popular understanding of creative process as one's internal heuristic act, one can look at it as a reasoning process that is guided by the relation of the individual to the outside. Creativity, then, emerges from the differences between the individual's will and those of others. The outcome is considered within the plurality of works created by many individuals. What contributes to this understanding of creativity from a designer's view has already been discussed. It is vagueness in sense perception, sagacity as the individual's incentive with it, and a relational view of the world that denies universal hierarchies where objects are classified according to pre-set notions. Creativity is a reasoning process where definitions can vary.

Not having a predetermined structure for thought does not imply the absence of reasoning. William James makes sagacity an indispensable part of reasoning that plays into creativity in much more flexible ways than those prescribed by the sciences. In the Pragmatist premise, reasoning builds on process and process builds on personal interaction with the object. It is contextual, based on experiences and habits, and does not conform to universal generalizations. Its rules are not finite as long as sagacity is practiced. Grounding definitions of thought in the creative process and the utility of the senses is the opposite of the conventional interactions of art with science, where creativity is being explained through scientific principles. All this prevails in a distinctive pedagogical standpoint, shared by Ross and Dow as well, where individuals are encouraged in their unique ways, which can only be represented in temporary and discardable conceptual structures.

Following this understanding, Ross and Dow's systems of abstraction demonstrate ways of reasoning, how to set up frameworks in a design process and apply rules exceptional to moments in the process. Their work shows a conscious manipulation of forms with the constraints that they establish. For example, Ross bases his analyses of photographs on spatial relations of particular diagonals. He traces geometric triangulations

66   *Early Beginnings*

on various portrait photographs showing them as composition lines. These lines mostly refer to the boundaries of the figures in the image, rather than a presumed center of mass. He usually selects one particular triangle and uses this to build a system that explores variations within that system. Figure 3.3 is one of Ross's finished analyses. The analysis illustrates a system of abstraction over a photograph of a woman. Most of the lines drawn take their reference from the image. For example, certain lines follow the outlines of the chair while some are tangential to the head. Also, the lines altogether belong in a system based on a formal relation, which is, in this case, a right triangle with the ratio of one of the sides to the hypotenuse as 1:2.

In the introductory booklet for an exhibition of his work in 1923, Ross explains his thought process:

> I then look at my subject and make up my mind which one of many possible diagonals will be the best one for the purpose. I draw that diagonal and another to balance it and reciprocal lines crossing the diagonals at right angles. These six lines will give me directions and angles of a single right angles triangle and are all I require.
>
> (1923, 4–5)

Based on this, the illustrations in Figure 3.3 speculate on how Ross builds up his system of abstraction for one example. The superimposed lines trace what Ross has drawn but without the knowledge of the original order that they were drawn in. They show a possible set of initial lines that start establishing a triangular guide. These lines, with the exception of the horizontal line, take their reference from the figure in the photograph. The horizontal line is arbitrarily placed but is the result of a perpendicularity rule that will help determine a right triangle. Ross first seems to establish a set of perpendicular lines that mostly take the image as reference. So far, this is similar to the motif of the perpendicular orthogonal lines in Dow's analyses. Simultaneously, a diagonal that traces the dress, and a secondary vertical line through the other arm of the chair follow. The spatial relation of the diagonal with the other lines establishes the basic angle for the triangular geometry

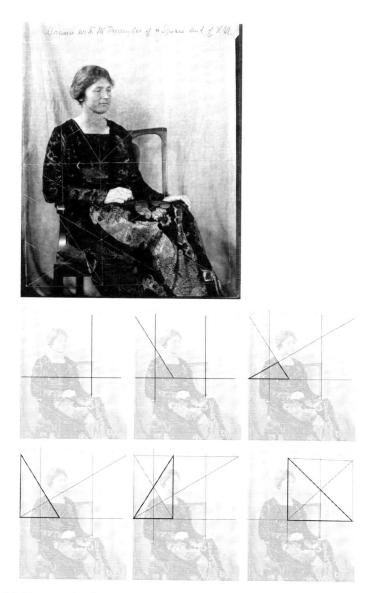

Figure 3.3 Photograph of woman seated in 3/4 pose with geometric analysis of triangles of a square and of XM, undated.

Note: Superimposed drawings by the author.
Source: Denman Waldo Ross Study Materials, box 30. Harvard Art Museums Archives, Harvard University, Cambridge, MA.

68   *Early Beginnings*

Ross aims for. The triangle is a right triangle of √4; the ratio of its short side to the hypotenuse is 1:2.

Ross's first lines mostly follow reference points from the image with the exception of the center horizontal line. It does not refer to anything in the figure (nor is it derived later on in his system of triangles) but it follows a perpendicularity rule. Its placement is arbitrary but the relationship is intended. It enables Ross to define the right triangle. Despite some arbitrary placement of lines, Ross tries to be consistent in his thinking:

> In producing the composition it is possible to modulate from the directions and angles of one triangle to those of another, if there is a good reason for doing so: but the systems combined must have one or more elements in common.
>
> (1923, 3)

Ross allows for variation as he sees it, but he wants to also continue using at least one rule, or one feature, consistently. Perpendicularity is one of these features. As he builds his system, the triangle that he derived from the initial lines becomes the basic element for the composition.

Later, Ross "modulate[s] from the directions and angles of one triangle to those of another." In a speculative order, the illustrations in Figure 3.3 show that he mirrors, rescales, and rotates the initial triangle. In the first one, Ross draws a diagonal that is perpendicular to the earlier one and, at the same time, tangential to the face. This produces the reciprocal of the √4 triangle. In the second one, he rescales (doubles) the original triangle to the implicit boundary of the frame and starts establishing a bordering frame for his analysis. In the third one, he draws a new diagonal and a vertical that mirror the last triangle, and maybe take reference from the figure underneath.

He produces a whole series of √4 triangles in similar manner. Nevertheless he allows for exceptions. In addition to the repeating triangles of √4, the caption above his analysis indicates a system of "triangles of a square" as well. This refers to the triangles shown in the last row of Figure 3.3. even though they are not actually triangles of a square. Ross has a secondary system of triangulation connected to the first. He presumes this is a √2 triangulation.

The Psychology for Basic Design 69

The assumed square has adjacent sides with a ratio of 2:√3. Ross constructs this based on the vertical line referencing the back of the chair and the existing triangular geometry. Following his description that this is a square, however, triangles in this portion of the analysis would be of √2. In any case, these comprise a variation from the √4 triangulation. It indicates to us that Ross interchanges geometries to his preference. He swaps visual rules, and the transformations he applies to them. It becomes more a design problem than an analysis.

Another example of variation in Ross's analyses is that he carries the same visual rules to other contexts. In the example in Figure 3.4, he switches to a different background image, this time a portrait of a man with a hat, and builds up a system with the same √4 triangles applied with various transformations of scale and orientation.

There are opportunities for being sagacious while applying the triangle rules. Ross's eye constantly picks out diagonals to draw new diagonals in a triangular relationship. He does this with mirrored or rescaled versions of the triangle that is the basis of the rule. Sagacity also applies at the initial level, when Ross was deciding on the first diagonals, hence the rule. His eye picks out parts that seem relevant then and there. Then, he manipulates the triangle, within the boundaries set by its geometric limitations but still flexibly, as he desires.

An entirely different geometry could also be set up using other spatial relations that abstract form relations from the same background figure. As the system develops with variations of initial rules, new spatial relations emerge as seen in the earlier example of Figure 3.3. Although the procedure in each example would be very personal, the point in trying out new ones is that in the end what emerges is more than just an analysis of a photograph, but a design. The pedagogical importance of these analyses is precisely this.

Dow's rules are much simpler than Ross's, but serve a similar purpose in setting up constraints. His "diagonals" are always horizontal or vertical in relation to the frame. His placing a line rule is specifically to pick out horizontal and vertical reference lines. The only two spatial relations are of parallel and perpendicular lines. Regarding landscape drawings, he refers to perpendicularity as the principle of opposition where vertical lines cut the horizon. Sometimes the vertical element is the frame itself.

Figure 3.4 Photograph of man with hat in profile with geometric analysis of rectangle √3 and drawn with the triangle of √3, undated.

Source: Denman Waldo Ross Study Materials, box 30. Harvard Art Museums Archives, Harvard University, Cambridge, MA.

The Psychology for Basic Design 71

However simplistic his system of rules is, he uses these abstract guidelines to demonstrate how to set up constraints accordingly with the context, and through these changing constraints how one can reason at the same time. John Masheck (1997, 5) calls Dow's underlying structures "empty diagrams." But these structures are not absolute. Apart from understanding given constraints through experimenting with the material and apparatus, one develops personal/individual constraints to guide the design process. Paul Klee's grids in *The Thinking Eye* (1961) are comparable to Dow's grids (Dow, 1997 [1899, 1920], 89) because Klee also refers to the grid as an underlying structure. Klee presents four grids together, the first of which displays, in his own words, "very primitive structural rhythm" (Klee, 1977 [1953], 22). Dow changes distances between lines and the number of lines in the grid. Like Dow, Klee changes the distances in between perpendicular lines in the second grid and there is a visible thickening of both the horizontal and vertical lines towards the center. In the third and fourth alternatives, Klee also allows for distortion in the frame and the perpendicular geometry of the units. In the third, individual units of the grid transform into quadrilaterals and in the fourth, curves are introduced. J. Abbott Miller writes, "Klee's pedagogical writings re-consider the grid as active, rather than passive" (Lupton and Miller, 1993, 9).

Froebel thought it necessary to distribute grids as supplements to the gifts. These grids came as lined boards and offered different-sized square units. Froebel's grid/network set a precedent for the pedagogical use of abstraction, especially regarding Dow's vertical and horizontal guidelines. Nevertheless, grids did not allow uncertainty as much as the frameworks described above do. Primarily this is because Froebel did not expect any manipulation of the grid in a visual thinking process. He encouraged the students to be guided by the lines in putting the planar forms together. In his book, Froebel provided examples of how this could be done. He arranged square planes neatly following the square units of the grid in symmetric or central compositions (Froebel 1902 [1899], Plates IV, IX). This is the same point from which Ross and Dow had started off. Yet, whereas Froebel had the rules of the grid set from the beginning, Dow changed the distances between the lines, and the number of lines, and Ross altered the sizes of the units on the same network, introduced angles, and selectively eliminated the units.

72 *Early Beginnings*

Compared to Ross and Dow's frameworks, Froebel's grid is very rigid. Tablets are arranged solely on their relation to the grid and their own geometry, that is a part of that grid. Even if there are offsets from the grid, they are often pedantic fractions like a quarter length or a half. This kind of utility only works as a counting system, hence the need for the entire set of lines even if they are not visually used. Ross's lines always serve a visual purpose even if momentarily. If there is no visual purpose, the lines are not there. One can say that Ross's grids and Froebel's grids had different efficiencies. Froebel's grid gave the basic unit, a square in one specific relation to a neighbouring replica, and showed all the combinations this provides. Ross's system showed the process with its varying possibilities at each moment. The efficiency required to keep the number of lines to only those necessary was collateral to the visual thinking process. The efficiency in Froebel's network, on the other hand, was the repetition of the same relationship set in the beginning. Its use was similar to that of Maratta's design paper. Moreover, for Froebel, drawing in the network involved understanding sizes and proportions of shapes. He was interested in cultivating the eye as a measurer (Froebel, 2001c [1899, 1902], 78). Froebel also gave examples of octagonal arrangements on the grid. Froebel (ibid., 78) wrote that these and other circular arrangements with the tablets are more advanced ways to use the grid. Even "more advanced" arrangements are based on the basic formal relationship in Froebel's network. These arrangements are still very much dependent on the same principles of the grid. They take its metrics as reference. In the end, Froebel's grid does not expand the design space. In a different way, we see the grid becoming an active tool in Dow's paintings and Ross's analyses.

Maratta's triangular grid and Ross's use of it are not very different from Froebel's approach to the grid. Ross does not explicitly mention its measure but uses the formal relations between its primitives. Design that is constructed on Maratta paper is connected to those relations in the grid. The deviation is that this grid carries a geometric bias different from the orthogonal one. Nonetheless, very simple shape relations are exercised. The pedagogical purpose in the use of these grids seems to be to show precursors to more active ones.

Off the grid, Froebel's tablets and other gift blocks still constitute a framework because of their defining geometry. In fulfilling the role of play

The Psychology for Basic Design   73

blocks, they show more than what the eye picks out. As explained by George Stiny (1980, 420), Froebel's kindergarten blocks illustrate how the framework is manipulated through perception of the hand's touch. Alignment of two rectangular blocks against the hand, using it as an edge, is tactile rather than visual. Sagacity permeates to the other senses. Ross and Dow do not explicitly talk about systems of reasoning that use senses other than the visual. At least, they promote hands-on experimentation with craft activities.

Pedagogical implications of abstraction in Ross and Dow's work are twofold. First, Ross demonstrates analysis of finished work. How to use that in a generative sense is not clearly articulated. There are no examples where the student makes an analysis and uses it generatively. The only exercises given to students involve finished frameworks such as Maratta's equilateral triangle grid to generate designs on it. And the Maratta grid does not connect to a prior context. This might be plausible in terms of avoiding any semantic bias on the students' part. However, there is a benefit in drawing up a dynamic grid for the purposes of understanding a work, and its elements, and reusing the elements to reconstruct it.

This advantage is also observable in Dow's system of abstraction for landscape drawings. A quick sketching exercise has the same effect, where students are given a time limit. They learn to pick out certain essential parts (there and then, changing from time to time, from person to person) to make a quick representation. Drawing vertical and horizontal axes, as well as framing the scene helps. These abstractions facilitate thinking about design on basic terms. This is apparent especially in Dow's work. He first lays the foundational structure (the abstract, that emerges as the pedagogical tool) and then works with it, reflectively, to create his painting over it. The abstraction works as a structure. More than Ross, Dow imagines the finished composition at the beginning.

Second, Ross's system of abstraction, even without the examples of students applying it, demonstrates a pedagogical tool to think with sagaciously. The framework helps Ross constrain his process. This is in terms of both understanding how constraints affect the process and in developing new ways to constrain it. When used dynamically, abstract guidelines allow for ambiguities to be observed. Instead of claiming there is order in everything, Ross shows he can create order in any context.

74   *Early Beginnings*

He chooses between various photographs and paintings, and he also establishes different triangle rules specific to each. He uses tools of abstraction to show his reasoning in design.

Frederick C. Moffatt, John Masheck, and Mary Ann Stankiewicz offer different viewpoints on the degree of formalism in Ross and Dow's works. Mostly, they consider Ross's formal methods to be too scientific in comparison with Dow's. Moffatt (1977, 91) observes Ross's "radical" attempt to free composition from "'the accidents of vision' so crucial to the Dow-Fenollosa formulations ..." Indeed, Ross himself had remarked that "[a]s we rise above the accidents of vision or of memory ... we discover that our knowledge of nature or life is a knowledge of Nature's consistency ..." (1901, 374). Despite statements such as this one that claim a direct link to consistent rules in nature, Ross's approach is milder than both what Moffat gives credit for and the scientific approach to design that came after Ross. This is a misunderstanding of Ross who also wrote statements with regards to the insignificance and irrelevance of what type of line is drawn as foundation: "It is not necessary, therefore to use either photographs or triangles" (1923, 4). Ross noted that it is simply "easier to get good compositions with triangles than rectangles," and that the right-angled triangle is "wonderful" as a module (ibid., 2). He does not have a grand theory of aesthetics as he writes down these reflections on his own process. We can accept that he was not idolizing any form in nature for purposes other than practical use. The significant concept in his work is the foundation, the underlying grid, or the frame, the ephemeral abstract tool. He allowed for free experimentation within these boundaries and left judgment of aesthetic value to the students.

As a follow-up on Moffat's remark on "accidents of vision," Masheck's presentation of Dow's position is similar to Ross's. Referring to Leonardo's "method of stimulating pictorial ideas by studying random spots on a wall for imagic suggestions," Masheck (1997, 4–5) writes: "Dow was out to suspend pictorial incident so as to bring forth image structure, the structure of forms, which, once acknowledged, might be refilled with freely appointed pictorial incident." What needs to be stressed here is that Dow too used ephemeral tools of abstraction. The pictorial incident in blurring blots of paint can also refer to the structures that he set up, temporarily. The significance of Ross and

The Psychology for Basic Design 75

Dow's work, and maybe not so much their grand theories about art or science, is that they used abstraction as a tool to understand and discuss the design process. In my opinion, they both represent a consciousness in the designer of being able to manipulate the intellectual tools and all the while recognizing perceptual variance.

Reviewing the influence of Ross and Dow's systems on art education, Mary Ann Stankiewicz cites a survey in art education published in 1908 by C. L. Boone. The survey shows that, as early as 1908, many art teachers had been using Ross and Dow's systems as "ends," and not as means (Stankiewicz 1988, 93). Ross and Dow had not presented an absolute resolution but suggested a technique that could be varied. It is possible that their legacies could have been either misinterpreted or marginalized in the scope of the survey. This short-sightedness is paralleled today in critical perspectives towards the use of computation in design. Visual rules, as the computational devices for reflecting with, are not there to impose design decisions but are rather instrumental in documenting processes. Computational devices are misconstrued as either threats to creativity or used solely as a means to an end with compelling stylistic results. In reviewing Ross and Dow's work today, it is meaningful to emphasize their insistence on the individual developing their own techniques by trying them out and observing others. The constraints that Ross and Dow introduced were pedagogical tools, of simple relations. They were not imposing rules to be followed exclusively, nor were they a visual style. Ross and Dow simply exemplified how relations could be set. The student was to explore within limits that are individually, designerly, set and can vary.

Bibliography

Adams, Henry. "William James, Henry James, John La Farge, and the Foundations of Radical Empiricism." *American Art Journal*, v. 17 (Winter 1985): 60–67.

Arnheim, Rudolf. *Visual Thinking*. Berkeley, CA: University of California Press, 1969.

Arnheim, Rudolf. *Art and Visual Perception*. Berkeley, CA: University of California Press, 1974 [1954].

Berkeley, George. *An Essay Towards a New Theory of Vision*. Dublin: printed by Aaron Rhames, for Jeremy Pepyat, 1709.

76 *Early Beginnings*

Boring, Edwin G. *A History of Experimental Psychology*. New York: Appleton-Century-Crofts, Inc., 1950 [1929].

Dow, Arthur Wesley. Sixth and last lecture in the course entitled "Modern Landscape Painting" given to the Board of Education, November 8, 1905. Arthur W. Dow Collection, Ipswich Historical Society Archive, Ipswich, MA.

Dow, Arthur Wesley. Draft for a talk given at Kindergarten Association in Philadelphia, February 15, 1906. Arthur W. Dow Collection, Ipswich Historical Society Archive, Ipswich, MA.

Dow, Arthur Wesley. *Theory and Practice of Teaching Art*. New York: Teachers College, Columbia University, 1912.

Dow, Arthur Wesley. Constructive art-teaching. Address before Western Drawing and Manual Training Association, Cincinnati, May 1, 1912. New York: Teachers College, Columbia University, 1913.

Dow, Arthur Wesley. Text for an exhibit at the conference of Fine Arts and Industrial Arts, February 21, 1914. Arthur W. Dow Collection, Ipswich Historical Society Archive, Ipswich, MA.

Dow, Arthur Wesley. "Talks on Appreciation of Art, No. I." *The Delineator*, (January 1915a): 15.

Dow, Arthur Wesley. "Talks on Appreciation of Art, No. III, Dark-and-Light." *The Delineator*, (July 1915b): 15.

Dow, Arthur Wesley. Letter to Henry Rodman Kenyon, 12 January 1915c. Ipswich Historical Society Archive, Ipswich, MA.

Dow, Arthur Wesley. "Talks on Appreciation of Art, No. IV, Color." *The Delineator*, (February 1916): 15.

Dow, Arthur Wesley. "Modernism in Art." *The American Magazine of Art*, v. 3, n. 8 (January 1917).

Dow, Arthur Wesley. *Composition: A Series of Exercises in Art Structure for the Use of Students and Teachers*. Berkeley, CA: University of California Press, 1997 [1899, 1920].

Dow, Arthur Wesley. Arthur Wesley Dow papers. Archives of American Art/Smithsonian Institution. [Microfilm reels 1208–1209, 1271, 1079, 3620, 1027, 1033–1034].

Dow, Arthur Wesley. An Explanation of Certain Methods of Art Teaching: Q & A. Ipswich Historical Society, Arthur W. Dow Collection, n.d. Arthur W. Dow Collection, Ipswich Historical Society Archive, Ipswich, MA.

Froebel, Friedrich. *Education by Development*. Trans. Josephine Jarvis. Grand Rapids, MI: The Froebel Foundation, 2001. [New York: D. Appleton and Company, 1899, 1902].

Froebel, Friedrich. *Pedagogics of the Kindergarten*. Trans. Josephine Jarvis. London:Routledge, 2001a. [New York: D. Appleton and Company, 1895].

Froebel, Friedrich. *The Education of Man*. Trans. W. N. Hailmann. London: Routledge, 2001b. [New York: D. Appleton and Company, 1888].

The Psychology for Basic Design   77

Fry, Roger. *Vision and Design*. London: Chatto & Windus, 1920.

Gavin, William Joseph. *William James and the Reinstatement of the Vague*. Philadelphia, PA: Temple University Press, 1992.

Green, Nancy and Jessie Poesch. *Arthur Wesley Dow and American Arts & Crafts*. New York: The American Federation of Arts, 1999.

Hofstadter, Richard. *Social Darwinism in American Thought*. Boston: The Beacon Press. 1962 [1944].

Itten, Johannes. *Design and Form: The Basic Course at the Bauhaus*. Trans. John Maass. New York: Reinhold Publishing Corporation, 1963.

James, William. "Does Consciousness Exist?" *The Journal of Philosophy, Psychology and Scientific Methods*, v. 18, n. 1 (1904).

James, William. *Principles of Psychology*. Cambridge, MA: Harvard University Press, 1983. [New York: Henry Hold and Company, 1890].

James, William. *Pragmatism*. New York: Dover Publications, Inc., 1995 [1907].

James, William. *A Pluralistic Universe: Hibbert Lectures on the Present Situation in Philosophy*. Lincoln, NE: University of Nebraska Press, 1996 [originally given in 1908 at Manchester College].

Klee, Paul. *The Thinking Eye*. Trans. Ralph Manheim. New York: G. Wittenborn, 1961. Klee, Paul. *The Pedagogical Sketchbook*. Trans. Sibyl Moholy-Nagy. New York: Frederick A. Praeger, Inc., 1977 [1953].

La Farge, John. *Considerations on Painting*. New York: The Macmillan Company, 1908.

Locke, John. *An Essay Concerning Human Understanding*. London: Rutland, 1993 [1689].

Logan, Frederick M. *Growth of Art in American Schools*. New York: Harper & Brothers, 1955.

Lupton, Ellen and J. Abbott Miller. *The ABC's of [Yellow Triangle, Red Square, Blue Circle]: The Bauhaus and Design Theory*. New York: The Cooper Union for the Advancement of Science and Art, 1993.

Mallgrave, Harry F. (ed.) *Empathy, Form and Space: Problems in German Aesthetics, 1873–1893*. Trans. Harry F. Mallgrave and Eleftherios Ikonomou. Santa Monica, CA: The Getty Center for the History of Art and the Humanities, 1994.

Masheck, John. "Introduction: Dow's Way to Modernity for Everybody." In Arthur Wesley Dow. *Composition*. Berkeley, CA: University of California Press, 1997, pp. 1–61.

Moffat, Frederick C. *Arthur Wesley Dow (1857–1922)*. Washington, DC: The Smithsonian Institution Press, 1977.

Naylor, Gillian. *The Bauhaus Reassessed: Sources and Design Theory*. London: The Herbert Press, 1985.

Nute, Kevin. "Frank Lloyd Wright and Composition: The Architectural Picture, Plan, and Decorative Design as 'Organic' Line-Ideas." *Journal of Architectural and Planning Research*, v. 4, n. 14 (Winter 1997): 271–288.

78 Early Beginnings

Ross, Denman W. "Design as a Science." *Proceedings of the American Academy of Arts and Sciences*, v. 21, n. 36 (March 1901): 357–374.

Ross, Denman W. Address on Design: Public Exercises at the Dedication of the Memorial Hall. Given at Rhode Island School of Design. Tuesday, November 24, 1903. In biographical and general information relating to Denman Waldo Ross, ca. 1880–ca. 1935. HUG 1753.400. Harvard University Archives.

Ross, Denman W. *A Theory of Pure Design: Harmony, Balance, Rhythm.* Boston: Houghton Mifflin and Company, 1907.

Ross, Denman W. *On Drawing and Painting.* Boston: Houghton Mifflin Company, 1912.

Ross, Denman W. *Experiments in Drawing and Painting.* New York: The Century Association of New York, Exhibition, November1923.

Ross, Denman W. Letter from Denman W. Ross to Edward W. Forbes, May 30, 1929. Harvard University Art Museums Archives, Edward W. Forbes files.

Ross, Denman W. Harvard University Art Museums Archives. Denman W. Ross Archival Materials.

Ross, Denman W. and Arthur W. Dow. "Architectural Education." *The Inland Architect and News Record*, v. 5, n. 37 (June 1901): 38.

Ross, Denman W., Edgar O. Parker, and S. Clifford Patchett. *Illustrations of Balance and Rhythm: For the Use of Students and Teachers.* Boston: W. B. Clarke Company, 1900.

Saranlı, Türel. "Temel Tasarımın Geçmişi ve Bugünü [Basic Design in Past and Present]." In Necdet Teymur and Tuğyan Aytaç-Dural (eds.) *Temel Tasarım/ Temel Eğitim* [Basic Design/Basic Education]. Ankara: ODTÜ Mimarlık Fakültesi Yayınları, 1998.

Singerman, Howard. *Art Subjects: Making Artists in the American University.* Berkeley, CA: University of California Press, 1999.

Stankiewicz, Mary Ann. "Form, Truth and Emotion: Transatlantic Influences on Formalist Aesthetics." *Journal of Art & Design Education*, v. 1, n. 7 (1988).

Stankiewicz, Mary Ann. "Rules and Invention: From Ornament to Design in Art Education." In Donald Soucy and Mary Ann Stankiewicz (eds) *Framing the Past: Essays on Art Education.* Reston, VA: National ArtEducation Association, 1990.

Stankiewicz, Mary Ann, Patricia M. Amburgy, and Paul E. Bolin. "Questioning the Past: Contexts, Functions, and Stakeholders in 19th-Century Art Education." In Elliot W. Eisner and Michael D. Day (eds.) *Handbook of Research and Policy in Art Education.* Mahwah, NJ: Lawrence Erlbaum Associates, Inc., Publishers, 2004.

Stiny, George. "Kindergarten Grammars: Designing with Froebel's Gifts." *Environment and Planning B*, v. 7 (1980): 409–462.

Stiny, George. *Shape: Talking about Seeing and Doing.* Cambridge, MA: MIT Press, 2006.

van Eck, Caroline. *Organicism in Nineteenth-century Architecture: An Inquiry into Its Theoretical and Philosophical Background*. Amsterdam: Architectura and Natura Press, 1994.

Whitehead, Alfred North. *Essays in Science and Philosophy*. New York: Philosophical Library, Inc., 1947.

Whitehead, Alfred North. *Process and Reality*. New York: The Humanities Press, 1955 [London: The Macmillan Company, 1929].

Whitehead, Alfred North. *The Concept of Nature*. London: The University Press, 1964 [1920].

Whitehead, Alfred North. *Science and the Modern World*. New York: The Free Press, 1967a [London: The Macmillan Company, 1925].

Whitehead, Alfred North. *The Aims of Education and Other Essays*. New York: The Free Press, 1967b [London: The Macmillan Company, 1929].

Whitford, Frank. *Bauhaus*. London: Thames & Hudson, 1984.

Wiener, Philip P. *Evolution and the Founders of Pragmatism*. Philadelphia, PA: University of Pennsylvania Press, 1972 [Cambridge, MA: Harvard University Press, 1949].

Wingler, Hans. *The Bauhaus*. Cambridge, MA: The MIT Press, 1969.

Worringer, Wilhelm. *Abstraction and Empathy*. Chicago: Elephant Paperbacks, 1997 [1908, 1953].

Part II
Looking to the Future

4 The Disillusioning Pasts of Basic Design

The Arts and Crafts movement in England and America was the persistent result of a general reaction to the mechanized ways of the developing industries. The art historian Charles Eliot Norton promoted the movement in Boston, the intellectual setting that created American Pragmatism. Local artists Denman Waldo Ross and Arthur Wesley Dow had been exposed to John Ruskin's theories and William Morris's work and were both involved in the movement. Their interest was pedagogical as well as for their own art works. Ross's "theory of pure design" at Harvard University had partially grown out of interactions with Arthur Wesley Dow, the local painter who separately developed a curriculum to teach "composition" in painting. After teaching in Boston and Ipswich, Dow taught at Teachers College in Columbia University from 1908 to 1922. The emphasis on techniques and how the process of creation relates to these techniques contributed to Ross and Dow's separate advocacy of the trainee's individual sensory experiences in design teaching. The ornamental and decorative arts also allowed Ross and Dow to isolate formal relationships and focus on the abstraction process in their pedagogical courses. Instead of de-emphasizing the ornament, a thing that is only visual, using it as a tool to understand how the visual and other material qualities play into the process of creative thinking is a progressive idea. Although a meaningful social context is something that plays itself out in the design process all the time, it will never literally translate to any visual aspect of form. Forms will be perceived through the context, and be meaningful in unique ways for each instance.

84　*Looking to the Future*

Ross and Dow's interest in decorative arts was combined with their exposure to the work of the Impressionists in Europe and curiosity for the arts of the Far East. They were among the first to show the Orientalist interest in America and through Ernest Fenollosa, at the Museum of Fine Arts in Boston, they were exposed to quite a lot of it. These relationships contributed to many aspects of their work, from being keen on a strongly sensory experience in the design process, and the use of different techniques in painting, to moving away from realistic representations and using minimalist and asymmetric aesthetics in understanding how paintings could be structured in abstract ways.

Ross and Dow's concerns with how design is done are more significant than their aesthetic choices and how they itemize principles for design. The principles they propose give clues to their understanding of the design process but are often not much more than other theories that have been proposed and used over time. Therefore, more than their fundamentals of design, as published in their magnum opuses *A Theory of Pure Design* and *Composition*, the book so far has looked at Ross's wallpaper exercises, photograph analyses, use of grids, general notes on organic form, and Dow's woodcut printing techniques as he learnt them from the Japanese, his ways of abstracting form relations in developing design ideas, and his general notes on education. Ross's work is significant for keeping the parts and wholes dynamic while Dow's work sees the impact of techniques on the design process. Both show ways to set up constraints through diagrams of relations between abstract forms. At the same time, they are aware of how personal engagement and the sensory experiences of the individual play into the design process and that these constraints change along the way. Ross and Dow together represent the launch of a tradition in design curricula which help the beginner students acknowledge designing as a personal reasoning process while they proactively learn about abstraction tools, sensory engagement and reflective thinking instead of pre-set categories for viewing the world.

The Arts and Crafts Movement of the late nineteenth-century movements preceded the twentieth-century avant-gardes in contending geometric canons. Understanding the role of material and techniques in

Disillusioning Pasts of Basic Design 85

design allowed for more spatial qualities to come through in designs. It also brought a new discussion of creativity that involved senses in thought processes as discussed by the Pragmatists. Denman Ross put emphasis on hands-on education in reaction to the idealist model: "Those old fashioned scholars, they don't know what it is to think in terms of physical effort and movement" (1903, 11).

This critical perspective dates back to earlier pedagogies. Early nineteenth-century child educators Johann H. Pestalozzi (1746–1827) and Friedrich Froebel (1782–1852) emphasized concrete experiences to stimulate senses and for individual development. Lists of "art-occupations" such as leather, metal, wood carving, modeling with clay, wax or plaster, printing, and textiles for Columbia University are in Dow's curriculum notes at Ipswich Historical Archives. This listing follows up on Froebel's occupations that actively involved the student with the gifts. The abstract two-dimensional analyses of Ross and Dow allowed mostly for the sagacity of the eye. Froebel and Dow's occupations engage both the hand and the eye. The gist of all these instances of hands-on learning is for the student to understand that creativity is a self-conscious process and not simply formal or material variance. This is much more important than asymmetries, or appreciating different visual cultures, even different materials as mentioned in other approaches above. Once individuality of each process is understood, variance is bound to happen.

There are no concrete examples of spatial exercises invented by Ross or Dow that encourage experimentation with tactile and visual qualities at the same time. Ross and Dow's work isolates vision and makes possible its misconception as formal inquiry. Their emphasis was primarily on developing the visual sense, as was common to most educational theories in the late nineteenth century. This common trend might have been because the drawback of pure intellectualism was apparent, and the newly recognized ambiguities of visual perception offered an answer. Perhaps this was also due to the fact that the visual history of humanity provided a more comprehensive background and a primacy to vision. The sense of touch had not yet been investigated much and only recently incorporated into psychology, and in psychology, the sense of vision "was the best known of the five senses" (Boring, 1950 [1929], 93). Boring (ibid., 110–113) discusses the sense of touch with due importance only

86 *Looking to the Future*

decades later. Nevertheless, perceptiveness always applied in tactility as well, and integrating the hand in design processes together with the eye could have especially extended Ross's theory to spatial inquiries and spread his impact to architecture.

Also evident in Ross and Dow's work, the shortcomings of trying to address uncertainties in design education lie in structuring the exercises given to the students. The answer to the question of what the student is going to walk away with from an exercise should be left open rather than being established as "a sense for balance, rhythm, or symmetry." The fallback onto having a set of timeless principles has often happened in the arts and architecture. We see it in a variety of instances from the mathematical ideals of the Renaissance to Owen Jones's *The Grammar of Ornament* (1986 [1856]), and Christopher Alexander *et al.*'s *Pattern Language* (1977), but also in the context of design education with the Bauhaus basic design tradition. The problem is apparent today in how designers interact with emerging technologies in their thought processes. Computation in the engineering sense compromises the plurality of thought with predefined and hierarchical structures. This is not surprising. Engineering objectives converge on feasibility, efficiency, and optimization, and rely on repeated elements. Embracing these values in design, looking from a strictly practical standpoint in the architectural profession is understandable but not sufficient at all in a profession that contributes to the society through much more than a recurring mechanical functionality.

4.1 Pure Design, Composition, and the Break with the Past

Ross and Dow's work shows us an attempt at applying the pragmatist premise for creative thinking – a self-conscious process carried out in individualized processes and with changing rules depending on the context and intent. The process only then makes use of perceptual uncertainties and allows for plurality.

The difficulty seems to be in maintaining the opportunities for students' unique perceptions while trying to establish a pedagogical agenda. At the least, the pedagogical method requires a consistent approach. The basic concepts used repeatedly to guide the processes in assignments could easily turn into deterministic principles. Ross and Dow's instrumental frameworks proposed for design students to use demonstrate mutual perceptiveness and reasoning as in William James's description, to a certain extent, but they stall before further exploration in times that follow them, maybe due to a supposed determinism. Furthermore, despite the attention they pay to the possibilities of variety, Ross and Dow mostly pursue the same set of frameworks – namely, the orthogonal and the diagonal line relations.

There is little evidence of student work to show the applied pedagogy of Ross and Dow. In-depth archival research is necessary to seek out educational outcomes that create varying systems and rules of abstraction based on what they propose. Otherwise, it is not possible to assess if Ross and Dow's demonstrations of setting up frameworks help instigate creative thinking. Additionally, there is little continuance of their pedagogy through their influence. So far, the 1908 survey that Stankiewicz (1988) cites does provide some information about their followers, but it rather proves these followers' misinterpretation of the method. Similarly, Arthur Pope (1929), one of Ross's students, who was a professor at Harvard, continued Ross's legacy but did so through creating a consistent set of principles in *The Language of Drawing and Painting*.

In England, another influential educator followed Ross's path. In *Vision and Design*, Roger Fry pointed out the harm that representation does to visual thinking and approved of Ross's abstract approach devoid of representational meaning: "Dr. Ross wisely restricts himself to the study of abstract and meaningless forms. The moment representation is introduced, forms have an entirely new set of values" (Fry, 1920, 21).

Stankiewicz (1988, 88) writes: "Thinking about abstract formal relationships, as Ross did, provided a theoretical base for critical theories such as Fry's which explained abstract art and argued for its aesthetic value." But Fry does not seem to have taken full advantage of the "meaningless" forms. Literature on Fry mostly agreed on his formalist approach to abstract art that runs contrary to changing values (Taylor, 1977; Lang, 1962). Indeed, Fry himself established ideal formal values: "One chief aspect of order in a work of art is unity" (1920, 20). He then went on to say that: "In a picture this unity is due to a balancing of the attractions of the eye about the central line of the picture" (ibid., 21).

88 *Looking to the Future*

Second, Ross and Dow did not break away from general notions such as balance, harmony and rhythm in talking about the basics. In spite of their approach where the principles and frameworks are personal and changing, balance, harmony, and rhythm inevitably bring them back to shared definitions and a general idealism in aesthetics.

The choice of the words, "pure" and "composition", in the titles of the most famous treatises by Denman Ross and Arthur Dow, *Pure Design* and *Composition*, seems in accord with the conservative view of aesthetics that largely governed art and architectural education in the nineteenth century. The words imply a sterile formalism that can be acquired only in a finite number of ways. The general view, dating back to the Renaissance and aspiring to Classical models, claimed harmony, rhythm, and balance as well as symmetry to be basic aesthetic principles. Idealized natural forms provided reference to these principles and their flat, geometric applications in art and architecture, as briefly mentioned in Chapter 3 in relation to organicism as well as in Chapter 1 with historical precedents for Ross's analyses. Nevertheless, there is an operative difference between these and Ross and Dow's works. Acknowledging the significance of each in its own right, it is possible to perceive Ross's "pure design" as a focus on abstract (meaningless) form and Dow's "composition" as a focus on the relations between these forms.

Art history marks the end of concentric ideals in nineteenth-century Western art and architecture with the "peripheric [asymmetric]" compositions of the European Avant-Garde (Rowe, 1953). This assessment also parallels the divide between two dominating traditions of the classical and the avant-garde in architectural education: the Beaux-Arts and the Bauhaus. Whereas the Beaux-Arts approach maintains the classical formalism based on the notion of types, the Bauhaus methodology, originated in 1919 in Weimar, Germany, is representative of the avant-garde and encourages individual expression. Basic design education is recognized today as the legacy of the Bauhaus. It is an opening curriculum of architecture education and consists of experimentation with material, abstract forms, and constrained abstract problems. A switch between the two traditions of architectural education can be specifically observed in American universities, such as at Harvard with the arrival of the influential Walter Gropius from the Bauhaus in 1937.

Disillusioning Pasts of Basic Design 89

Ross and Dow's interest in Japanese art had introduced them to the notion of asymmetric compositions in the late nineteenth century. Their designs and paintings displayed asymmetry, as exemplified in the previous chapters. More importantly, however, their pedagogical undertaking was not merely about a stylistic inquiry. They were acting in a period of developments in hands-on learning approaches to child education and the Arts and Crafts movement. Both of these associations had influenced their techniques in achieving dynamic designs. Their – then unusual – formal arrangements served to show the students possibilities for various form relations and to encourage them to think about unique processes to develop these. Probably because of this background, Ross and Dow even reacted to the formal expressionism that the European avant-gardes brought. Both of them, having visited Europe in late nineteenth century, had been friendly with the post-Impressionist, pointillist, and Fauvist circles. Nevertheless, Ross's conservative side came through in a letter to one of his students. His student was actively involved in founding the first modern art exhibition at the Harvard Fogg Art Museum. Ross (1929) wrote in a letter to him:

> When it comes to the post-impressionists I have no interest in their theory and no interest in their work ... The key note of post-impressionists is self-expression; with the will to be unprecedented and shocking. The result is lawlessness ... As for your going to Harvard Square and starting an exhibition and sale of examples of contemporary art because precedence has been given to other and better things at the Fogg Museum; it is a silly and ridiculous example of self-assertion and self-expression on your part.

Considering their own progressive position in America, Ross and Dow's caution and apathy may be interpreted to their credit. Their theories had methodological components that had grown out of the history mentioned above. Dow knew they were ahead of the avant-gardes. In a letter to his painter friend Henry Rodman Kenyon, Dow (1915c) wrote:

> Perhaps you saw [the American impressionist Charles] Vezin's article on flat tones. It sails into modernism very severely.

90 *Looking to the Future*

> Mrs. Mowbray-Clark is up here [in New York City] lecturing – a kind of blow, or advertisement of the Davies-Henri crowd [Arthur B. Davies and Robert Henri were among the first to exhibit independently from the National Academy of Design in 1907 (Schwartz, 1984, 49)]. They have just discovered the things Fenollosa and Ross talked about 20 years ago!

Münsterberg taught a course on aesthetics at Harvard (Frank, 2008a). William James had initially invited Münsterberg to Harvard although did not always share his views. In James's inquiries about reasoning, sensations were unique and experimentation served to reveal this rather than demoting them to anticipated ideals. These inquiries were concurrent with the "pure design" course instigated by Denman Waldo Ross in the Architecture and Fine Arts Department at Harvard. Ross's course, where the student was learning to develop his own understanding of forms, stood out at the school in what was otherwise a Beaux-Arts tradition of education. Ross taught at Harvard from 1899 until his death in 1935, so most of his teaching pre-dated Walter Gropius's arrival from the Bauhaus.

In the end, Ross's fear of lawlessness proved wrong. The design education that emerged from that avant-garde work, as well as from the work of those who followed Ross and Dow, was instead the opposite. Restrictive frameworks somehow re-emerged. This investigation is not intended as an extensive historical research of what followed Ross and Dow. Still, it is important to show that the ideas at the end of the nineteenth century did not see further exploration in basic design education. In thinking about abstract forms and form relations, Ross and Dow were unique in pushing towards a pragmatist approach and anticipating twentieth-century modern thought. However, their influence did not persist, partially because their work sustained the visual qualities of the old styles and perhaps partially due to their characters. On the contrary, the twentieth-century moderns introduced new visual material that captivated interest through the years, but slipped back to rigid ways of thinking about design. The next section draws on some historical threads of related pedagogical interest that fall short in appropriating perceptiveness in creative thinking.

4.2 Formal Idealism

Asymmetric line arrangements were exciting because they broke away from strict patterns prescribed in a holistic and static worldview. Expanded knowledge of organic systems and psychology at the time supported this formal change. The change was only an indication of the new understanding of a dynamic world and dynamic creative processes. However, it was also very easy to lapse back to the static view if these forms became the new ideals.

Jay Hambidge, in his investigations on dynamic symmetry, geometrically described how to construct asymmetric forms like the spiral. In explaining how to construct a shell spiral, Hambidge (1960 [1932], 39) wrote:

> [T]he line EC is a mean proportional between the lines EA and EB. E is the pole or eye of the curve. The lines AB and DC are drawn through the pole at right angles to each other. When three lines EA, EC, and EB are in this position, the lines AC and CB form a right angle at C.

These descriptions were instructive for designers in a new way. All the same, Hambidge's intention to legitimize classical works like Greek pottery through this sort of scientific talk gave this pursuit a different meaning. He consistently based his geometric descriptions on proportions like Fibonacci ratios and validated these newly appreciated non-concentric forms through their existence in an idealized nature. His shell spiral is an example of fractals popular in bibliographies today in computing as well as aesthetics. Fractals show that organic growth could be understood in categories, as a model for complexity and variation. But this kind of recursive complexity and variation is diametrically opposed to allowing for perceptiveness in creative thinking. Here, there is no variance in parts; the only variance is in scale and Euclidean transformations. Abandoning symmetries and concentric compositions is only a formal exercise that brings in idealized forms once again, now appreciated as dynamic.

Another lead to a stagnant view is in claiming origins for asymmetric forms. In the early 1920s, many looked to ethnic art for the formal

92 *Looking to the Future*

variety that classical works usually lacked. In a way, this was no different from Ross and Dow's interest in Japanese art. Critics at the time noted a parallel between Japanese and primitive arts in terms of the consciousness of the abstract. One critic was Roger Fry who paralleled "the bushman silhouettes of cranes" with Japanese screen drawings. His observation of this parallel relied on the silhouette being perceived as a maximal whole as in the Impressionists' "attempt to get back to that ultra-primitive directness of vision" (1920, 63–64).

At the same time, there was a tendency to identify global concepts as the motivation behind these abstract forms. As an example, the influential Mexican painter and educator Adolfo Best Maugard listed seven basic motifs in primitive art as the beginnings of a new language of form: the spiral, the circle, the half-circle, the s curve, the wavy line, the zigzag, and the straight line. Best Maugard (1926) wrote: "The suggestions and rules that we will follow are simple and easily understood by everyone. They are quickly grasped and retained in the mind of the student," referring to the seven simple motifs. He considered these to be "fundamental, and a few rules to follow, and these, once in the student's memory, will enable him to make an infinite number of combinations and designs ..." (ibid., 1–2). He aimed to identify a finite global vocabulary of basic elements and saw design as the combinatory arrangement of these elements.

Suitable to an educational purpose, playing with these simple primitives could also have served to understand the works in a particular style. An educational agenda to teach the basics as preparation for more complex systems in the future goes back to systems like Owen Jones's set of principles in *The Grammar of Ornament* (1986 [1856]). Later, Laszlo Moholy-Nagy's reference to Raoul Francé's "seven biotechnical elements" was along the same lines (Moholy-Nagy, 1947 [1928], 46). The "seven biotechnical elements" were the basic constructional units of the physical world: crystal, sphere, cone, plate, strip, rod and spiral (screw). Moholy-Nagy approached design from a functional point of view, and believed that these elements were the key forms for efficient designs. Interestingly, he excluded these elements from the production of plastic form (sculpture). He wrote that sculpture is understood in "plastic development – and not as the application of geometric and biotechnical elements." Nonetheless, outside of the realm of plastic art, his view of design was functionalist. He claimed the seven elements he coined as "the basic technical elements of the whole world" (ibid., 46).

To draw parallels to a more recent but similar approach from a computational context, one can refer to Christopher Alexander's work on building an urban and architectural pattern language. Alexander (1964, 136–173) observes primitive urban settlements to develop a form language based on predetermined components. His basic vocabulary exceeds the sets of seven elements given above and is not purely formal like them. Yet, in principle, it carries out the same motivation of establishing a system of construction from a predefined set of units. In his work, Alexander also shows the hierarchical arrangement of the construction. By explaining how the physical elements of a village emerge, he implies design to be a hierarchical organism. These methods are useful in design but also setting the limits of physical space and restricting design to what is already known. Abstract shapes and concepts then work as the convenient basic vocabulary in theoretical languages of form, rather than exploratory tools. These design approaches take credit from a functionalist viewpoint whereas in the context of basic design education, top-down reduction severs variation in experience.

4.3 Psychology as the Science of Aesthetics

The history of basic design, as mostly associated with the Bauhaus, is traced back to early nineteenth-century child educators, Johann H. Pestalozzi and Friedrich Froebel. Both Pestalozzi and Froebel are known for their reformative approach to education with emphasis on hands-on learning. They defined the character of the kindergarten. Johannes Itten, who set up the basic design course at the Bauhaus a century later, was a former kindergarten teacher himself. Itten's *Vorkurs* was not light-hearted with regards to psychological aspects of designer thinking. His empathy exercises were famous. But it was his contemporaries at the VKhUTEMAS (the Higher Artistic-Technical Studios), another design school in Moscow, who were more determined to involve sensory experience in design. In 1920, an architect and the key figure at the Moscow School, Nikolai Ladovsky organized a basic course on the psychoanalytic method and set up a psychotechnics laboratory for measuring factors such as "attention,"

94   *Looking to the Future*

"memory," "perception measurements," and "spatial and motor abilities." Contemporary with the Bauhaus, Ladovsky's design school in Moscow attempted to integrate psychology into design education. Ladovsky led a group of Russian avant-gardes at the VKhUTEMAS (the Higher Artistic-Technical Studios) to set up the basic design curriculum. All this was inspired by the work of Hugo Münsterberg, the German psychologist who was the head of the experimental psychology laboratory at Harvard University as early as 1890. Not much has been written on how the developing field of psychology affected the Russian avant-garde. Detailed descriptions of what the laboratory equipment at the VKhUTEMAS really showed also do not exist. But the implication of this kind of set-up for the pedagogical program was towards converging sensory experiences into a shared corpus rather than exploring the differences.

The key idea behind the basic design course at VKhUTEMAS was to integrate sensory experience into design education and design thinking. Nonetheless, Ladovsky's larger agenda was to base the integration on the psychological response of individuals to form and space. For this, he referred to contemporary experimental findings in perceptual psychology at the Harvard Psychological Laboratory. Architectural historian Anatole Senkevitch (1983, 80) explains that rather than stylistic clues, the results of perceptual experiments led to "organizing the design process and cultivating in the designer a dynamic three-dimensional manner of conceiving architectural form and space."

The motivation does not seem to be a formalist one. The projects that were produced in the course focused on mostly three-dimensional arrangements of abstract forms. The relevant literature does not describe the pedagogical methods applied, but the projects look similar to basic design assignments elsewhere. Moreover, comparable to the approaches of Froebel, Dow and the Bauhaus, the school was a conglomerate of various arts and crafts faculty (Cooke, 1995, 71).

All the same, Ladovsky claimed in 1926 that his interest in perceptual experiments was focused on "the laws of perception." This marks a diversion from the pedagogical focus on variation in thinking. Ladovsky and his colleagues sought a formal explanation of the observer's bodily sensations in relation to the perceived object or space. Ladovsky later set up a laboratory at the VKhUTEMAS to accompany the basic course with experiments in visual perception. Detailed descriptions of what the laboratory equipment really showed and their scientific origins do not exist. In the laboratory existed five apparatuses to measure linear, planar, volumetric, angular, and spatial magnitudes. The implication of this kind of a set-up for a pedagogical program seems to be towards converging sensory experiences into a shared corpus rather than exploring the perceptual differences. Ladovsky had hoped that the results that came out of the laboratory would be an answer to "the absence of any agreed terminology even among specialists" and would clarify misunderstandings in qualitative assessment of architectural space (1991, 26).

Interestingly, the set-up was inspired by the work at the experimental psychology laboratory at Harvard (ibid., 26). This is a direct connection to the Pragmatist line of thought instigated by William James and others. James had established the laboratory at Harvard, but at the time of its influence on the VKhUTEMAS, the German psychologist Hugo Münsterberg was heading it. Senkevitch stresses that in the first decade of the twentieth century, this laboratory was unique in the world (1983, 91). Münsterberg was initially invited from Germany to join the Harvard faculty by William James in 1890. His PhD dissertation entitled *Activity of the Will* (1888) and his position against scientific idealism in German psychology had prompted the invitation. Later on, Münsterberg diverged from his action theory, or rather, opened up to other disciplines, including law. As he became a public figure in America, James, among others, fell out with him. Senkevitch concedes in correspondence that Münsterberg's interests were found to be too diffuse, but also suggests that "Germans at Harvard" were then (in the aftermath of war) given a hard time. Münsterberg's *Psychology and Education* essay elucidates his later position that "categories of psychology" should not be forced on "the values of our practical life" and that the role of psychology in teaching is minimal unless the students are given charge of "having ideals and acting in response to them" (cited in Münsterberg, 1922, 312).

Even if he was highly reliant on Münsterberg's theories, Ladovsky overlooks this warning and focuses on deterministic aspects of the application of psychology in education. His position was that "psychotechnics" could give artists a solid foundation for "scientifically correct"

96   *Looking to the Future*

achievements. The geniuses were always recognized as default cases that achieve such results intuitively (cited in Ladovsky, 1991 [1926]).

Despite the direct link to Harvard, in the end, the VKhUTEMAS diverged from the main line of thought stipulated here with Ross and Dow. The divergence is twofold. First, Ladovsky's approach focused on the relation between the object and the observer rather than the designer's thought activities. Second, the first-hand attempt at science was presented as the only option to engage in the differences in perception. Instead of a reasoning process that benefits from these differences, the rational approach at VKhUTEMAS emphasized the deterministic use of spatial perception in design.

Ladovsky and his colleagues theorized about perceptual experience in order to pursue its shared meaning in composition. Senkevitch makes connections to the theory of empathy, based on the fact that they attempted to link the architectural object to the observer through bodily sensations (1983, 79). Their approach is far from a design pedagogy that would allow the designer to be active through his or her sense perception. This is also very different from Ross and Dow's way of thinking. The intellectual tools that Ross and Dow provide with abstract forms and form relations allow for perceptual variations in the thought process. The mind-set at the VKhUTEMAS puts more value on communicating meaning through shared precepts than variation. Communication cannot be the prime agenda of creative thinking as it relies on common concepts. Ladovsky's attempt to define these concepts beforehand places the designer in a more passive position than a thinker.

4.4 Visual Education

Similar directions ensued in the Bauhaus legacy with the influences of Gestalt psychology as well as the Vienna Circle from the late 1920s onwards. The Gestaltists proposed a set of rules for perception, such as the laws of proximity, similarity, closure, good continuation, and symmetry. These helped, more than the pedagogical ideas in the basic design curriculum, but a particular visual and formal exploration that was later deemed a style. Additionally, contemporary to the beginnings of the Gestalt effect on the Bauhaus, its faculty developed close relations with the logical positivists, such as the philosopher Rudolf Carnap and the sociologist Otto Neurath in the Vienna Circle. Even though both Carnap and Neurath were interested in visual thinking, their primary agenda to unify life around the same set of building blocks reduced experience to logical propositions and engulfed perceptual variation. This agenda was a revolt against the one-sided politics that dominated at the time, and later coupled with the functionalist view that embraced technology as a universal liberation of mankind from subjective criteria. Within all this, the affiliation between the Bauhaus and the logical positivists resulted in reducing basic design instruction to a basic vocabulary of forms that are universally shared. Ramifications continued as the avant-gardes fled to America before the Second World War, and as the impact of Gestalt psychology on the arts grew in the 1940s.

The connection between the VKhUTEMAS and the Bauhaus is not only through Kandinsky's transfer from Moscow to the Bauhaus in 1923. The impact of the psychological research at Harvard on the VKhUTEMAS also connects the two schools historically (Lang, 1991, 71–72). The Bauhaus lived under the influence of positivist thought shortly after the time of the rationalist and scientific approaches at the VKhUTEMAS. This was partially in association with Gestalt psychology. The Bauhaus faculty was in touch with Gestalt psychologists Wolfgang Köhler and Rudolf Arnheim in the late 1920s. That epistemological connection continued even after the Bauhaus resettled in America.

The influence was also sourced elsewhere. A mutual interest between the Bauhaus and a group of scientists in Vienna formed as early as 1926 (Neurath, 1926, 209–211). Known as the Vienna Circle, the scientists, who included the philosopher Rudolf Carnap and the sociologist Otto Neurath, were propagating a scientific conception of the world. Their manifesto set out a unified structure in science through applying modern logical analysis to experience.

> Since the meaning of every statement of science must be statable by reduction to a statement about the given, likewise the meaning of any concept, whatever branch of science it may belong to, must be statable by step-wise reduction to other concepts, down to the concepts of the lowest level which refer directly to the given.
>
> (Neurath, 1973 [1929], 309)

98 *Looking to the Future*

The *concepts of the lowest level* were experiences. But they were reduced in form to the basic elements in a language that would unite all knowledge in one common definition.

The method, logical positivism (or modern empiricism), started out with reliance on only what is directly experienced. But this reliance was rather on what is defined as experience. Empirical material was classified as propositions that are to be the building blocks of the larger structure of knowledge. The classification eliminated uncertainties as all experience is reduced to concepts from the start. As William James had written earlier, "The real units of our immediately-felt life are unlike the units that intellectualist logic holds to and makes its calculations with" (James, 1920, 287). Thought is an extension of perception, and does not have discrete parts. This understanding is important from a design point of view because design is a reasoning process that is not solely based on preconceived knowledge. Design creativity should not conform to an intellectual structure that severs the variation in experience. Logical positivists, for their own political reasons, neglected the changes in social, cultural, and physical contexts. The unified system of knowledge that they proposed eliminated these in order not to affect experience, and they excluded uncertainties.

Neurath's attempt at visual education revealed his understanding of the potentials of perception. Otto Neurath had recognized the non-linear perceptual qualities of visual representations. He seemed to appreciate the changing part–whole relations in visual perception as opposed to the linearity in verbal languages. He showed that overlapping parts of a shape are simultaneously conceived unlike in a linear reading of a series of the parts that are separately laid out, and stated: "Visual statements and verbal statements are different and not translatable element by element" (Neurath, 1996, 330). In accompanying images to this depiction and statement, Neurath showed that overlapping parts of a shape, in this case, a boy stick figure walking through a door, are simultaneously conceived, unlike in a linear reading of a series of the parts that are separately laid out.

Neurath was interested in the efficiency of visual perception. This helped his larger motivation for educating the masses with a common language. ISOTYPE, the international picture language he proposed, was

Disillusioning Pasts of Basic Design 99

built from simple visual elements that combine to acquire more complex figures. For example, the symbol for coal imprinted on the symbol of a worker was to represent a coal-worker (Chapel, 1996, 181). Visual descriptors for "worker" and "coal" together build the descriptor for "coal-worker" in Neurath's ISOTYPE. In the end, Neurath's visual method provided a symbolic language that was much more depictive than verbal, but no more "vague." Neurath was after clarity.

The attempt at a general structure for a unified science extended to a unity of life in Rudolf Carnap's "logical construction of the world" (1969). This included art, which was otherwise a metaphysical statement of mood and spirit (Neurath, 1973 [1929], 307). The logical positivists were happy to be associated with the Bauhaus as this link supported their position. Historian of science Peter Galison (1990) writes that the formalist motivations of the Vienna Circle and the Bauhaus were in parallel. Walter Gropius had even invited Carnap to lecture at the Bauhaus in 1929. Galison notes that at the visit, Carnap was particularly impressed by the basic design course, especially Kandinsky's work (1990, 737–738).

By the time Carnap visited the Bauhaus, the basic design course had changed in philosophy. Itten had left in 1923, around the time that Kandinsky arrived from Moscow. The Bauhaus faculty was already mostly thinking along the same lines as the logical positivists. Kandinsky's form theory was an example of this similarity. He had reduced the plane to three primary forms: triangle, square, and circle (Kandinsky, 1994 [1923], 500; 1979 [1926], 74). These geometric elements were rather like logical propositions as building blocks for all other forms. Kandinsky's reductionist approach was earlier referenced in relation to Ross and Dow's frameworks. Ross and Dow also established basic rules to build up their framework from. Nonetheless, Ross's utilization of triangles and Dow's application of perpendicularity were part of thought processes that are self-conscious of perceptual variation. Neither of them established any forms as universally basic building blocks. Kandinsky's approach led back to the primitive elements as those identified by Best Maugard. Unity of life required getting rid of uncertainty, and in the parallel case of the Bauhaus, this resulted in visual idealism.

Carnap immediately saw a similarity in Kandinsky's elements with axiomatized geometry, the model which Carnap himself considered to

100 *Looking to the Future*

construct all philosophy (Galison, 1990, 737–738). The geometrical building up from the elementary suits the logical positivist agenda just as much as Neurath's visual language did. Galison quotes Bertrand Russell to illustrate the constructional program that Carnap might have had in mind:

> Unlike other conceptual systems, a constructional system undertakes more than the division of concepts into various kinds … it attempts a step-by-step derivation or 'construction' of all concepts from certain fundamental concepts, so that a genealogy of concepts results in which each one has its definite place.
>
> (cited in Galison, 1990, 733)

This description summarizes the construction in two steps, namely dividing and hierarchically arranging discrete concepts. Nevertheless, the step-by-step construction in design does not work in divisions or hierarchies. Rather, as in Ross's analyses, it follows unique paths. The basic element, that is a visual rule, varies according to formal transformations or is entirely replaced with other rules. There are no discrete parts to the process that are defined beforehand as universal elements.

Starting in the late 1920s, the pedagogical agenda of training students as individual thinkers had changed into a different educational plan at the Bauhaus. Bauhaus had a renewed relation with the technologies of the time. Especially under the directorship of Hannes Meyer, the Bauhaus operated more like a research laboratory where solutions were sought for an already defined problem: architecture and design were to integrate the economic and technical efficiency of the production world. The application of technological resources in architecture is very similar to the interaction with technologies in architecture schools today. One difference is that Meyer had openly dismissed aesthetics, completely replacing it with functionalism: "Building is not an aesthetic process … building is only organization: social, technical, economic, mental organization" (cited in Whitford, 1984, 180).

Form production is an important part of the integration of technology and design that goes on today. But between the formalisms of the techniques and expressionistic mannerisms, aesthetics is not sufficiently

Disillusioning Pasts of Basic Design 101

pursued as an ongoing discussion. When the aesthetic discussion dies, the utility of senses and uncertainties seem to be lost along with it. The point that Meyer's Bauhaus missed, and a lot of designers miss today, is that aesthetics as a practice of perceptiveness is imperative, not only to beautify the world but more to serve in the crucial role in criticism. The later Bauhaus misconstrued the idea of involving the visual sense as an active part in creative thinking. In parallel with the logical positivists, their vision was subsumed by intellectualism and focused on logical thinking. The pedagogy that aims at unique and self-conscious individuals was for the large part abandoned.

Gropius, milder in his functionalist approach than Meyer, was still hopeful that ambiguities would persist throughout the interaction with new methods:

> Only by constant contact with advanced technology, with the diversity of new materials and new methods of construction, is the creative individual able to bring objects into a vital relationship with the past, and to develop from that a new attitude to design ...
>
> (Gropius, 1984 [1926], 206)

However, the positive meaning dramatically shifts when this new attitude is mostly the understanding that the built environment consists of machines and vehicles constructed exclusively with "primary forms and colors comprehensible to everyone" (ibid., 206). According to Gropius, there was only one way to interact with advancing technology and that was to accept its determination.

When European intellectuals migrated to America before the Second World War, the Bauhaus resettled at the University of Chicago. At that time, the Bauhaus faculty was associated with the agenda of the American philosopher Charles Morris. They also got involved with Gestalt psychology as interpreted by Rudolf Arnheim and Gyorgy Kepes who, like the logical positivists, instituted gestalts (wholes) as visual propositions. In Morris's perspective, the general program of the New Bauhaus joined the American intellectual tradition following Dewey's Art as Experience. Nevertheless, Morris's continued interest in the Vienna Circle and "the reduction of all utterances to protocol sentences" and the

102 *Looking to the Future*

call for talking about art "in the language of scientific philosophy" departed from Dewey (cited in Galison, 1990, 748). Reducing art to a logical language meant that it lost its visual component. If its thought were restricted to a closed system, the artistic process would become indifferent to perceptual variation. "The language of art" held the potential to reflect the consistencies in the visual and aesthetic quality of art, but as Morris matched creative thinking process to "scientific philosophy," all perceptual aspects involved became auxiliary.

To talk about design as reasoning, but without confining it to a linguistic and logical structure, lost interest in the post-Bauhaus context and has not resurfaced much apart from a few exceptions. Ross and Dow's pragmatist push was one of the earliest attempts to talk about design as such. Although more than a century old, because of its dual character that embodied reasoning and artistic sensibility at the same time, this short-lived attempt sheds more light on possible methodologies for a holistic design pedagogy than the idealist tradition that followed.

Bibliography

Alexander, Christopher. *Notes on the Synthesis of Form*. Cambridge, MA: Harvard University Press, 1964.

Alexander, Christopher. *The Timeless Way of Building*. New York: Oxford University Press, 1979.

Alexander, Christopher, et al. *A Pattern Language: Towns, Buildings, Construction*. New York: Oxford University Press, 1977.

Alofsin, Anthony. *The Struggle for Modernism: Architecture, Landscape Architecture, and City Planning at Harvard*. New York: W. W. Norton & Company, 2002.

Arnheim, Rudolf. *Visual Thinking*. Berkeley, CA: University of California Press, 1969.

Arnheim, Rudolf. *Art and Visual Perception*. Berkeley, CA: University of California Press, 1974 [1954].

Arnheim, Rudolf. *The Split and the Structure: Twenty-eight Essays*. Berkeley, CA: University of California Press, 1996.

Best Maugard, Adolfo. *A Method for Creative Design*. New York: Alfred A. Knopf, 1926.

Blake, Casey Nelson. "The Perils of Personality: Lewis Mumford and Politics after Liberalism." In Robert Hollinger and David Depew (eds.) *Pragmatism: From Progressivism to Postmodernism*. Westport, CT: Praeger, 1995, pp. 88–106.

Disillusioning Pasts of Basic Design 103

Blake, Casey Nelson. "Afterword: What's Pragmatism Got to Do with It?" In Joan Ockman (ed.) *The Pragmatist Imagination: Thinking About Things in the Making*. New York: Princeton Architectural Press, 2000, pp. 266–271.

Boring, Edwin G. *A History of Experimental Psychology*. New York: Appleton-Century-Crofts, Inc. 1950 [1929].

Burzan, Jacques. *A Stroll with William James*. New York: Harper & Row, 1983.

Carnap, Rudolf. *The Logical Structure of the World*. Trans. Rolf A. George. Berkeley. CA: University of California Press, 1969. [Original German edition, *Der Logische Aufbau der Welt*, 1928].

Cassirer, Ernst. *The Problem of Knowledge: Philosophy, Science and History since Hegel*. Trans. William H. Woglom and Charles W. Hendel. New Haven, CT: Yale University Press, 1950.

Chapel, Enrico. "Otto Neurath and the CIAM – The International Pictorial Language as a Notational System for Town Planning." In Elisabeth Nemeth and Friedrich Stadler (eds.) *Encyclopedia and Utopia: The Life and Work of Otto Neurath (1882–1945)*. Dordrecht: Kluwer Academic Publications, 1996, pp. 167–182.

Cooke, Catherine. *Russian Avant-garde Theories of Art, Architecture and the City*. London: Academy Editions, 1995. Dewey, John. *How We Think*. Boston: D.C. Heath & Co. 1910.

Dewey, John. *Experience and Education*. New York: Collier Books. 1963.

Dewey, John. *Art as Experience*. New York: Perigee, 1980 [1934].Dow, Arthur Wesley. Sixth and last lecture in the course titled "~~Modern~~ Landscape Painting" given to the Board of Education, November 8, 1905. Arthur W. Dow Collection, Ipswich Historical Society Archive, Ipswich, MA.

Dow, Arthur Wesley. Draft for a talk given at Kindergarten Association in Philadelphia, February 15 1906. Arthur W. Dow Collection, Ipswich Historical Society Archive, Ipswich, MA.

Dow, Arthur Wesley. *Theory and Practice of Teaching Art*. New York City: Teachers College, Columbia University, 1912.

Dow, Arthur Wesley. "Constructive Art-teaching." Address before Western Drawing and Manual Training Association, Cincinnati, May 1, 1912. New York City: Teachers College, Columbia University, 1913.

Dow, Arthur Wesley. Text for an exhibit at the conference of Fine Arts and Industrial Arts, February 21, 1914. Arthur W. Dow Collection, Ipswich Historical Society Archive, Ipswich, MA.

Dow, Arthur Wesley. "Talks on Appreciation of Art, NO. I." *The Delineator* (January 1915a): 15.

Dow, Arthur Wesley. "Talks on Appreciation of Art, NO. III, Dark-and-Light." *The Delineator* (July 1915b): 15.

Dow, Arthur Wesley. Letter to Henry Rodman Kenyon, 12 January 1915c. Ipswich Historical Society Archive, Ipswich, MA.

104 *Looking to the Future*

Dow, Arthur Wesley. "Talks on Appreciation of Art, No. IV, Color." *The Delineator* (February1916): 15.

Dow, Arthur Wesley. "Modernism in Art." *The American Magazine of Art*, v. 3, n. 8 (January 1917).

Dow, Arthur Wesley. *Composition: A Series of Exercises in Art Structure for the Use of Students and Teachers*. Berkeley, CA: University of California Press, 1997 [1899, 1920].

Dow, Arthur Wesley. Arthur Wesley Dow papers. Archives of American Art/ Smithsonian Institution. [Microfilm reels 1208–1209, 1271, 1079, 3620, 1027, 1033–1034].

Dow, Arthur Wesley. An Explanation of Certain Methods of Art Teaching: Q & A, Ipswich Historical Society, Arthur W. Dow Collection, n.d. Arthur W. Dow Collection, Ipswich Historical Society Archive, Ipswich, MA.

Efland, Arthur D. *A History of Art Education: Intellectual and Social Currents in Teaching the Visual Arts*. New York: Teachers College Press, 1990.

Eisner, Eliot W. *Educating Artistic Vision*. New York: The Macmillan Company, 1972.

Farmer, John David and Geraldine Weiss. *Concepts of the Bauhaus: The Busch-Reisinger Museum Collection, Introduction, Exhibition Catalogue and Handlist of the Bauhaus Research Collection, April 30–September 3, 1971*. Cambridge, MA: Harvard University Press, 1971.

Findeli, Alain. "The Bauhaus Project: An Archetype for Design Education in the New Millenium." *The Structurist*, n. 39–40 (1999–2000).

Frank, Marie. "Denman Waldo Ross and the Theory of Pure Design," *American Art*, v. 22, n. 3 (Fall 2008a), 72–89.

Frank, Marie. "The Theory of Pure Design and American Architectural Education in the Early Twentieth Century," *Journal of the Society of Architectural Historians*, v. 67, n. 2 (June 2008b), 248–273.

Froebel, Friedrich. *The Education of Man*. Trans, W. N. Hailmann. London: Routledge, 2001a. [New York: D. Appleton and Company, 1888].

Froebel, Friedrich. *Pedagogics of the Kindergarten*. Trans. Josephine Jarvis. London: Routledge, 2001b. [New York: D. Appleton and Company, 1895].

Froebel, Friedrich. *Education by Development*. Trans. Josephine Jarvis. Grand Rapids, MI: The Froebel Foundation, 2001c. [New York: D. Appleton and Company, 1899, 1902].

Fry, Roger. *Vision and Design*. London: Chatto & Windus, 1920.

Galison, Peter. "Aufbau/Bauhaus: Logical Positivism and Architectural Modernism." *Critical Inquiry*, n. 16 (Summer 1990): 709–752.

Gropius, Walter. *The New Architecture and the Bauhaus*. New York: Museum of Modern Art, 1936.

Gropius, Walter. "Dessau Bauhaus – Principles of Bauhaus Production [March 1926]." In Frank Whitford, *Bauhaus*. London: Thames & Hudson, 1984. pp. 205–207.

Hambidge, Jay. *Practical Applications of Dynamic Symmetry*. New York: The Devin-Adair Company, 1960 [1932].

Hartsthorne, Charles. "The Parallel Development of Method in Physics and Psychology." *Philos Sci*, v. 4, n. 1 (October 1934).

Hillier, Bill, et al. "Space Syntax." *Environment and Planning B*, v. 3 (1976): 147–185.

Hillier, Bill. *Space is the Machine: A Configurational Theory of Architecture*. Cambridge: Cambridge University Press, 1996.

Hollinger, Robert and David Depew. *Pragmatism: From Progressivism to Postmodernism*. Westport, CT: Praeger Publishers, 1995.

Husserl, Edmund. *Edmund Husserl's Origins of Geometry: An Introduction by Jacques Derrida*. Trans. John P. Leavey, Jr. New York: Nicholas Hays, 1978 [Original *Revue Internationale de Philosophie*, v. I, n. 2, 1939].

Itten, Johannes. *Design and Form: The Basic Course at the Bauhaus*. Trans. John Maass. New York: Reinhold Publishing Corporation, 1963.

Jaffee, Barbara. "The Abstraction Within: Diagrammatic Impulses in Twentieth Century American Art, Pedagogy, and Art History," vol. I. PhD dissertation, The University of Chicago, 1999.

James, William. "Does Consciousness Exist?" *The Journal of Philosophy, Psychology and Scientific Methods*, v. 18, n. 1 (1904).

James, William. *A Pluralistic Universe*. New York: Longmans, Green, and Co,. 1920.

James, William. *Principles of Psychology*. Cambridge, MA: Harvard University Press, 1983. [New York: Henry Hold and Company, 1890].

James, William. *Pragmatism*. New York: Dover Publications, Inc., 1995 [1907].

James, William. *A Pluralistic Universe: Hibbert Lectures on the Present Situation in Philosophy*. Lincoln, NE: University of Nebraska Press, 1996. [Manchester College, 1908].

Jarzombek, Mark. *The Psychologizing of Modernity: Art, Architecture, and History*. Cambridge: Cambridge University Press, 2000.

Jonas, Hans. *The Phenomenon of Life: Toward a Philosophical Biology*. Evanston, IL: Northwestern University Press, 2001 [1966].

Jones, Owen, *The Grammar of Ornament*. London: Studio Editions, 1986 [London: Day and Son, 1856]).

Kandinsky, Wassily. *Point and Line to Plane*. New York: Dover Publications Inc., 1979 [1926].

Kandinsky, Wassily. *Complete Writings on Art*. New York: Da Capo Press, 1994a.

Kandinsky, Wassily. "Bauhaus, 1919–1923 [1923]." In *Complete Writings on Art*. New York: Da Capo Press, 1994b, pp. 498–507. Klee, Paul. *The Pedagogical Sketchbook*. Trans. Sibyl Moholy-Nagy. New York: Frederick A. Praeger, Inc., 1977 [1953].

Klee, Paul. *The Thinking Eye*. Trans. Ralph Manheim. New York: G. Wittenborn, 1961.

106 *Looking to the Future*

Ladovsky, Nikolai. "The Psycho-Technical Laboratory of Architecture, 1926." In Andreas C. Papadakis, Catherine Cooke and Justin Ageros (eds.) *Architectural Design: The Avant-Garde Russian Architecture in the Twenties*. London: St Martins Press, 1991.

Lang, Berel. "Significance or Form: The Dilemma of Roger Fry's Aesthetic." *The Journal of Aesthetics and Art Criticism*, v. 2, n. 21 (Winter 1962): 167–176.

Lang, Jon. "Design Theory from and Environment and Behavior Perspective." *Advances in Environment, Behavior, and Design*, v. 3 (1991): 53–101.

Langer, Susanne. *Philosophy in a New Key: A Study in the Symbolism of Reason, Rite and Art*. Cambridge, MA: Harvard University Press, 1942.

Lipps, Theodor. *Psychological Studies*. New York: Arno Press, 1973 [c. 1926].

Logan, Frederick M. *Growth of Art in American Schools*. New York: Harper & Brothers, 1955.

Lupton, Ellen and J. Abbott Miller. *The ABC's of [Yellow Triangle, Red Square, Blue Circle]: The Bauhaus and Design Theory*. New York: The Cooper Union for the Advancement of Science and Art, 1993.

Mach, Ernst. *The Analysis of Sensations: and the Relation of the Physical to the Psychical*. Trans. C. M. Williams. New York: Dover Publisher, 1959.

Mallgrave, Harry F. (ed.) *Empathy, Form and Space: Problems in German Aesthetics 1873–1893*. Trans. Harry F. Mallgrave and Eleftherios Ikonomou. Santa Monica, CA: The Getty Center for the History of Art and the Humanities, 1994.

Marshall, Henry Rutgers. "The Relation of Aesthetics to Psychology and Philosophy." *The Philosophical Review*, v. 1, n. 14 (January 1905).

Martin, Marianne W. "Some American Contributions to Early Twentieth-century Abstraction." *Arts Magazine*, v. 10, n. 54 (June 1980): 158–165.

Marx, Leo. *Lewis Mumford: Prophet of Organicism*. No. 2 Working Paper in STS. Cambridge, MA: MIT Press, 1990.

Moholy-Nagy, Laszlo. *The New Vision*. New York: George Wittenborn, Inc., 1947 [1928].

Mumford, Lewis. *The Brown Decades: A Study of the Arts in America 1865–1895*. New York: Dover Publications, Inc., 1931.

Mumford, Lewis. *Roots of Contemporary American Architecture*. New York: Reinhold Publishing Company, 1952 (2nd edn, 1956). Munevar, Gonzalo. *Radical Knowledge: A Philosophical Inquiry into the Nature and Limits of Science*. Indianapolis, IN: Hackett Publishing Company, 1981.

Münsterberg, Margaret. *Hugo Münsterberg: His Life and Work*. New York: D. Appleton and Company, 1922.

Naylor, Gillian. *The Bauhaus Reassessed: Sources and Design Theory*. London: The Herbert Press, 1985.

Neumann, Eckhard (ed.) *Bauhaus and Bauhaus People: Personal Opinions and Recollections of Former Bauhaus Members and Their Contemporaries.*

Trans. Eva Richter and Alba Lorman. New York: Van Nostrand Reinhold Company, 1970.

Neurath, Otto. "Das neue Bauhaus in Dessau." *Aufbau*, v. 11–12, n. 1 (November–December 1926): 209–211. Neurath, Otto. "Visual Representation of Architectural Problems." *Architectural Record*, v. 82 (July 1937): 56–61.

Neurath, Otto. "Der Wiener Kreis, [1929]." In Otto Neurath, *Empiricism and Sociology*. Ed. Marie Neurath and Robert S. Cohen. Boston: D. Reidel Publishing Company, 1973. pp. 301–318.

Neurath, Otto. *Unified Science: The Vienna Circle Monograph Series*. Ed. Brian McGuinness. Trans. Hans Kaal. Dordrecht: Reidel Pub. Co.,1987.

Neurath, Otto. "Visual Education: Humanisation Versus Popularisation." In Elisabeth Nemeth and Friedrich Stadler (eds.) *Encyclopedia and Utopia: The Life and Work of Otto Neurath (1882–1945)*. Dordrecht: Kluwer Academic Publications, 1996, pp. 245–335.

Nute, Kevin. "Frank Lloyd Wright and Composition: The Architectural Picture, Plan, and Decorative Design as 'Organic' Line-Ideas." *Journal of Architectural and Planning Research*, v. 4, n. 14 (Winter 1997): 271–288.

Ockman, Joan (ed.) *The Pragmatist Imagination: Thinking about Things in the Making*. New York: Princeton Architectural Press. 2000a.

Ockman, Joan. "Pragmatism/Architecture: The Idea of the Workshop Project." In Joan Ockman (ed.) *The Pragmatist Imagination: Thinking about Things in the Making*. New York: Princeton Architectural Press, 2000b, pp. 16–23.

Papanicolaou, Andrew C. and Pete A. Y. Gunter. *Bergson and Modern Thought: Towards a Unified Science*. Chur, Switzerland: Harwood Academic Publishers, 1987.

Papert, Seymour. *Aesthetics in Science*. Ed. Judith Wechsler. Cambridge, MA: MIT Press, 1978.

Piaget, Jean and Bärbel Inhelder. *The Child's Conception of Space*. New York: W. W. Norton & Company, 1967 [Original in French 1948, first published in English 1956].

Pope, Arthur. *The Language of Drawing and Painting*. Cambridge, MA: Harvard University Press, 1929.

Pope, Arthur. *Art, Artist, and Layman: A Study of the Teaching of the Visual Arts*. Cambridge, MA: Harvard University Press, 1937. Putnam, Hilary. *Representation and Reality*. Cambridge, MA: The MIT Press, 1988.

Rajchman, John. "Another View of Abstraction." *Abstraction: Journal of Philosophy and the Visual Arts*, n. 5. (1995).

Robinson, Richard. "Ambiguity." *Mind*, v. 198, n. 50 (April 1941): 140–155.

Rorty, Richard. *Contingency, Irony and Solidarity*. Cambridge: Cambridge University Press, 1989.

Ross, Denman W. "Design as a Science." *Proceedings of the American Academy of Arts and Sciences*, v. 21, n. 36 (March 1901): 357–374.

108 *Looking to the Future*

Ross, Denman W. Address on Design: Public Exercises at the Dedication of the Memorial Hall. Given at Rhode Island School of Design. Tuesday, November 24, 1903. Biographical and general information relating to Denman Waldo Ross, ca. 1880–ca. 1935. HUG 1753.400. Harvard University Archives.

Ross, Denman W. *A Theory of Pure Design: Harmony, Balance, Rhythm.* Boston: Houghton, Mifflin Company, 1907.

Ross, Denman W. *On Drawing and Painting.* Boston: Houghton Mifflin Company, 1912.

Ross, Denman W. *Experiments in Drawing and Painting.* New York: The Century Association of New York, Exhibition, November1923.

Ross, Denman W. Letter from Denman W. Ross to Edward W. Forbes, May 30, 1929. Harvard University Art Museums Archives, Edward W. Forbes files.

Ross, Denman W., Edgar O. Parker, and S. Clifford Patchett. *Illustrations of Balance and Rhythm: For the Use of Students and Teachers.* Boston: W. B. Clarke Company, 1900.

Rowe, Colin. "Book Review, Talbot Hamlin, Forms and Functions of Twentieth Century Architecture." *Art Bulletin,* v. 35 (June 1953): 169–174.

Samson, Miles David. *German-American Dialogues and the Modern Movement Before the "Design Migration," 1910–1933.* Ann Arbor, MI: Bell & Howell Company, 1988.

Santayana, George. *The Philosophy of George Santayana.* Ed. Paul Arthur Schlipp. Evanston, IL: Northwestern University, 1940.

Santayana, George. *The Sense of Beauty.* New York: Dover Publications, Inc., 1955 [New York: Charles Scribner's Sons, 1896].

Santayana, George. *The Letters of George Santayana: Book One, [1868]–1909.* Ed. William G. Holzberger. Cambridge, MA: The MIT Press, 2001 [New York: Scribner, 1955, 1986].

Schön, Donald. *The Reflective Practitioner.* Aldershot: Arena, 1991.

Schopenhauer, Arthur. *The World as Will and Representation.* Trans. E. F. J. Payne. Indian Hills, CO: Falcon's Wing Press, 1958.

Schwartz, Constance. *The Shock of Modernism in America: The Eight Artists of the Armory Show.* Roslyn Harbor, NY: Nassau County Museum of Fine Art, 1984.

Senkevitch, Anatole. Trends in Soviet Architectural Thought, 1917–1932. Cornell University: unpublished PhD dissertation, 1974.

Senkevitch, Anatole. "Aspects of Spatial Form and Perceptual Psychology in the Doctrine of the Rationalist Movement in Soviet Architecture in the 1920s." *VIA Architecture and Visual Perception,* v. 6 (1983), 79–115.

Simon, Herbert A. *The Sciences of the Artificial.* Third edition. Cambridge, MA: The MIT Press, 1996 [1968].

Stafford, Barbara Maria. *Artful Science: Enlightenment, Entertainment and the Eclipse of Visual Education.* Cambridge, MA: The MIT Press, 1994.

Stankiewicz, Mary Ann. "Form, Truth and Emotion: Transatlantic Influences on Formalist Aesthetics." *Journal of Art & Design Education*, v. 1, n. 7 (1988).

Stankiewicz, Mary Ann. "Rules and Invention: From Ornament to Design in Art Education." In Donald Soucy and Mary Ann Stankiewicz (eds.) *Framing the Past: Essays on Art Education*. Reston, VA: National Art Education Association, 1990.

Stiny, George. "Kindergarten Grammars: Designing with Froebel's Gifts." *Environment and Planning B*, v. 7 (1980): 409–462.

Stiny, George. "How to Calculate with Shapes." In Erik Antonsson and Jonathan Cagan (eds.) *Formal Engineering Design Synthesis*. New York: Cambridge University Press, 2001, pp. 20–64.

Stiny, George. *Shape: Talking about Seeing and Doing*. Cambridge, MA: The MIT Press, 2006.

Taylor, David G. "The Aesthetic Theories of Roger Fry Reconsidered." *The Journal of Aesthetics and Art Criticism*, v. 1, n. 36 (Autumn 1977): 63–72.

Van Eck, Caroline. *Organicism in Nineteenth-Century Architecture: An Inquiry Into Its Theoretical and Philosophical Background*. Amsterdam: Architectura and Natura Press, 1994.

Vohringer, Margarete. Avant-garde and Psychotechniques: On the Convergence of Science, Art and Technology in Nikolai Ladovsky's Psychotechnical Laboratory at the VChUTEMAS, Moscow, 1926. PhD dissertation, 2003.

Weber, Nicholas Fox. *Patron Saints: Five Rebels who Opened America to a New Art, 1928–1943*. New York: Alfred A. Knopf, 1992.

Whitford, Frank. *Bauhaus*. London: Thames & Hudson, 1984.

Wiener, Philip P. *Evolution and the Founders of Pragmatism*. Philadelphia, PA: University of Pennsylvania Press, 1972. [Cambridge, MA: Harvard University Press, 1949].

Wingler, Hans. *The Bauhaus*. Cambridge, MA: The MIT Press, 1969.

Wittkower, Rudolf. "The Changing Concept of Proportion." In *Idea and Image: Studies in the Italian Renaissance*. New York: Thames and Hudson, 1978, pp. 109–123.

Worringer, Wilhelm. *Abstraction and Empathy*. Chicago: Elephant Paperbacks, 1997 [1908, 1953].

5 Computational Design Foundations[1]

Knowledge, skills, and attitudes are the three components of competence to which learning objectives of educational curricula extensively refer. At a first glance, computation in an architectural education curriculum may easily be categorized under skills simply because there is a technical characteristic attributed to its use in design. It is often associated with optimization methods to improve the economic factors of a design. Moreover, technology is usually understood as something to be applied. It offers techniques and tools, often developed by experts from another field. Nevertheless, this understanding is changing. The technologies have become widespread, open source, and manageable by an increasing number of experts from the field of design. Even if computation in design often requires skills to effectively operate a digital device or construct an elegant algorithm, it is also very much interrelated with knowledge that is ideally internalized as computational thinking and enables the individual to perform computation in design. It is also interrelated with attitudes that are required to judge when and why to do computational design. However, the subject matter of attitudes in the context of learning computational thinking deserves more attention than the scope of this book can offer.

This chapter sets out what may constitute a computational foundation for the learning of design thinking. This sketch of a proposal is twofold. The first part is the concept of employing the methodological devices of repetition and variation to deal with and organize complexity. The second is the concept of employing formal devices to talk about design. Both have precedents in the hundred-year-old approaches

112 *Looking to the Future*

illustrated in the pedagogical methods developed by Denman Waldo Ross and Arthur Wesley Dow. Below is yet another case for the first from a few hundred years earlier. The focus is on geometric patterns from Islamic architecture to demonstrate the rich applications of repetition and variation as an understanding of basic design. In addition to the stone or woodcarving, glazing and tiling skills applied in the craft of making these patterns, there is also a knowledge of design and, arguably, of computation, especially with regards to the geometries involved. Hence, these patterns teach us not only how to do but also how to think, and once understood, vary that thinking.

In the first year of my architectural education at Middle East Technical University, there was something compelling for me in designing geometric patterns on paper using just a compass and a ruler. The instructors of our Graphic Communication course had invited Ömür Bakirer, an art historian and architectural conservationist, to show us the basics of geometrically constructing Seljuk patterns. We were then expected to repeat a few existing patterns to train for the later phase: to come up with a new pattern on our own. Our guest speaker had pursued the idea that these patterns are constructed on circle grids very early on (Bakirer, 1981). A class of one hundred students, we drew on Scholler paper, with 4H and 2B pencils, meticulously brushing off the remnants of the eraser as we struggled with calculating the precision required to make the ends of lines meet and the circles touch one another just on one point. The lightly drawn guides that I had to produce as an invisible layer of directives then seemed to be the core of many things I say about design processes today. I remember applying a similar idea to a design project I did in the studio the same year. While critiquing plan drawings for the project, one of my professors exclaimed: "Let your guidelines be a little more visible once in a while!" He was implying that I should make the most of the system that I devised to organize the volumes and that it actually becomes a part of the design rather than an invisible layer that did not carry through to the final product. He later became a mentor.

Having started the book with Denman Ross's drawings on Maratta's grid papers, and the horizontal and vertical lines that Dow emphasized as organizational axes in any visual frame captured in painting and

Computational Design Foundations   113

photography, and Paul Klee stretched while talking about grids, I can vouch for the common feature in all: they are devices to lay the grounds for repetitive order in works of art and design. The grounds for repetitive order is similar to people aligning with a curb or a wall while queuing up. The curb provides a reference for order that each member of the queue repetitively takes into consideration while positioning oneself in relation to another member in the queue. Even in queues, there are inevitable variations, differences in distances between members, in proximity to the said curb, or the direction in which a member is facing. Hence, although these guides evoke order, they do not limit every aspect. Repetition also provides a base for comparison of two things. In repeating instances, we seek features that differ among the similarities. I think that we appreciate repetition more than we would like to admit. Even when we oppose it, we are in fact relying on it. But this reliance is rather on its absence that allows us to identify differences. This is what captivated my attention in drawing the Seljuk patterns years ago, or at least in my memory of drawing them, and is the subject matter of the section below.

5.1 Organizing Complexity: Variations in Repetition

We appreciate repetition. It allows us to recognize – or even to think that we wondrously discover – the new and the different amidst similarities. Whereas repetition implies consistent relations of similar parts, differences challenge these relations and stimulate our interpretive capacity towards recognizing multiple, unique but still meaningful, wholes. Dialogues that arise from repetition and variation characterize a good design. The aim here is to draw attention to a centuries-old visual design with a repetitive quality that resonates with computational iteration while it finds its character in variations that result from seeking and seeing different relations.

Repetition is common to many art forms. The literary world offers, in widely available contemporary resources on grammar, composition and literary terminology, a broad range of technical categories of repetition as rhetorical devices. These categories as well as notions of disordered rhythm and defamiliarization from early literary formalism (Shkolovsky, 1991, [1925]) are, to some extent, of interest to those who wish to articulate

114 *Looking to the Future*

what repetition implies for the visual arts. Surprisingly, perhaps because of the wide range of its media, the artistic world does not present such a common analysis of repetition techniques. Nonetheless, repetition often finds its artistic counterpart in rhythm. And spatial rhythm, as an organizational phenomenon, is widely accepted as an experiential treat and an invaluable trait in modernist art and architecture. Rasmussen's handbook of Modernist values in architecture (1959) is a key resource for this understanding. There is also a considerable amount of current literature that recognizes rhythm in visual designs and architectural space. Writings range from rigorous scholarly approaches such as the comprehensive *rhythm analysis* of urban environments (Lefebvre, 2004), or discussions of the role of redundancy in perceiving space (Lawson, 2001) to popular architecture blogs illustrating desired architectural spaces old and new with compositional repetitions. Sometimes, even if outside the realm of music, definitions of rhythm include movement and time. Within the scope of this text, the only movement in time required to observe the rhythm is that of the viewer's gaze. Rhythm is referred to as any perceived totality of repetitions and variations in a finished visual design.

Talking about repetition is an essential part of contemporary architectural design education, especially at the foundational level. As aspiring designers learn about design thinking, they begin to understand how and why one establishes relations between parts towards creating the larger meaningful whole. When we ask why a part of design is so, answers expose its relations to other parts: the arches above the windows mimic the section of the ceiling vault. Sometimes answers refer to parts from a broader external context: the arch of the window is a structural requirement to span an opening of that size.

In most good designs, we seek and find wholes. In designs where all relations are unique, a sense of the whole is lost. Unique relations between parts are only appreciated when there are repeating relationships at other levels. In Pollock's paintings where individual paint drops seem to have been accidentally placed, we seek and appreciate a larger whole for the entire canvas, calling out visual patterns. Alternatively, we refer to the entire set of the artist's similar paintings acknowledging his process of making. Pollock's bodily performance

Computational Design Foundations   115

provides a consistent reference for the paint drops across all his paintings.

Repetition, as essential as it is for design, is not always straightforward to perceive and to conceive. First, repetition of parts, which can be shapes as well as features or relations, is almost never monotonous in good designs. Parts do not necessarily repeat exactly to be deemed repetitious. Hence there is variation, and the notion of rhythm that encompasses both. The line between an exact copy and something similar is blurred. Our perception of what repeats helps us establish what parts are in the first place. Still, some parts may be deemed repetitious due to some of the smaller repeating parts within. Parts within wholes thus vary.

Let us assume that we generally perceive wholes, and may call them parts if we associate them with a larger entity. The repeating parts from different wholes help us relate these wholes to one another. Parts are similar at various scales and this similarity helps us connect parts to one another at these levels. Parts that are similar to one another seem to belong together. Second, a compositional whole does not begin and end in the object but expands to its environment also. For example, a soda bottle is a compositional whole in itself but also could be considered a part in a larger compositional whole when the consumer is holding it in their hand or it is among many similar bottles organized side by side on the market shelf. Contexts multiply our perception of part-whole relations.

5.1.1 Variation: The Visually Computable Counterpart to Repetition

In design education at the foundational level, students struggle with making decisions. Creativity is difficult when one has not yet developed a sense of how to set up a temporarily constrained environment that allows you to make decisions, one at a time and with implications on other decisions. If one can control relations, it is possible to make choices that implicate the whole. Creativity in design is more dependent on context than its counterpart in the arts.

Conventionally we have come to understand computation as the act of counting identity relations, which also passes as copying or repeating a set

116 *Looking to the Future*

relation. Stiny (2006) unconventionally reflects on this type of processes as zero dimensional because relations between parts are never questioned and set beforehand. Parts in digital computation are in fact primitives that cannot be divided into unprecedented smaller parts. Stiny, by contrast, draws attention to part relations that are technically called embedding. In higher-than-zero dimensional entities, parts are allowed, are infinitely many, and are decided on, temporarily, by the eye of the beholder. The eye embeds unprecedented parts in wholes. Decompositions change from person to person, from context to context, hence the potential for variation. Figure 5.1 shows alternative parts cut out from a circle. Once we identify parts as we see fit, we can count and copy them. In the third and fourth decompositions in Figure 5.1, there is two of each unique part whereas in the fifth, there are six. There is yet another level of identity relations here. Although different in shape, these five alternatives are particularly derived from the same constrained decomposition structure that is the key player in the text below.

The repeated relations make design computable in the zero dimensional way. Nonetheless, good designs also display a variance among parts, and the creative idea often exists in recognizing this variance among similarities. The variance is not only to successfully address the multiple contexts inherent in any design problem. Limiting the discussion to abstract and visual designs only, it is also due to the very nature of visual thinking where the eye composes and decomposes parts and wholes in different ways, as seen in Figure 5.1. The designer and the viewer appreciate the multitude of ways of relating to the work. Variation should be seen as an opportunity to create. Following in Stiny's footsteps, the indeterminacy in the involvement of the eye indicates that design computability is

Figure 5.1 Various decompositions of a shaded circle.

visual. Being visually computable implies that seeing complements repetition.

As it turns out, the visual interplay of repetitive and varied parts in design is a centuries-old problem in architectural design. One instance, which will be the focus of this section, is the geometric patterns extending over the surfaces of Seljuk (and more generally medieval Islamic) architecture and are based on repeating circles. Signifying infinity and continuity, these designs display a strong repetitive quality. They are repetitive not only in the endless iteration of units, but also because they conform to a style by reiterating certain motifs. Similar forms across geography help us identify them as what they are but this repetitive quality is well balanced with pattern variety as most are unique.

The geometric ornaments in Islamic architecture show variation over time and geography. They cover a larger domain within which the star-shaped Seljuk patterns comprise a particular geographical and temporal frame. The patterns of concern here are specific to the central and south-eastern regions of Asia Minor and the culture of eleventh–thirteenth-century Islam in that region. Rather than being a historical study, this investigation focuses on visual composition in these patterns and its geometric construction.

5.1.2 Seljuk Patterns: Repetitions of Constraints and Variations Upon Sight

A uniform field of interlocking circles, drawn simply on any surface using a compass and nothing more, is the underlying guide to construct various geometric relations of stars, convex polygons, and straight lines. These shapes emerge when the artisan's eye connects intersection points with new lines. The circle grid, usually based on the repetitive relation of two circles that pass through the other's center, also known as *vesica piscis*, ensures the unity of the overall structure as well as the style that sets these ornaments apart from others. It also yields to creative varia-tion as the artisan visually constructs the lines that eventually form unique patterns. Arguably, these patterns, with their constrained variety,

118 *Looking to the Future*

illustrate the basics of design, and are relevant for establishing a direct link between computation and design.

Design problems and solutions are always unique, as each design is ideally consistent and relevant in its context. In the particular case of the medieval Anatolian architectural ornaments, the motivation and the limitations of the design are very much defined by the social dynamics of the era (Bakirer, 1981; Mülayim, 1982). The period saw the rise of philosophical Islam. Figurative decoration was not permissible, so ornamentation on stone portal façades or on wooden minbars from the interiors was only geometric. The common motifs are variations of what is known as the "infinity motif" or the "star motif." In these motifs, large architectural surfaces are covered with repetitive patterns extending to the edges.

The patterns are constrained due to the expectations of the patrons and the belief system of their time. They are also a part of a more elaborate scheme of abstract art that decorated mostly portals of public buildings, side panels of tombs and grilles used for privacy indoors. The architecture of the period, especially in the region, displayed a mystic symbolism in volumetric organization. The ornamentation supplemented the stereotomy. There is an extensive literature on the meanings of these ornaments (Ogel, 1966) but these remain beyond the scope and pedagogical interest of this book.

Despite the common knowledge of the flow of mathematical and scientific knowledge from medieval Eastern manuscripts to the West, elaborate mathematics was not common knowledge among the medieval craftsmen. They knew how to implement shape construction practically but did not necessarily know the mathematics behind it. It is thought that the craftsmen worked with geometry experts as early as the eleventh century and had visual instructions in how to efficiently divide and unite wood panels without the use of any calculation device (Özdural, 2000). Materiality and constructive knowledge of geometry are key to Bakirer's explanation as well. She extends her investigations with more case studies (Bakirer, 1992) and provides evidence that artisans carved interlocking circles on the stone on site (Bakirer, 1999). These served as the guidelines to apply designs directly onto the material with both the repetitions and the variations that emerged out of the processes of visual thinking and making. Bakirer's description of the process provides the

Computational Design Foundations 119

basis for a richer computational understanding of the design of units in relation to the overall design of a panel. These patterns are then a step-by-step construction that entails much seeing on behalf of the designer-craftsman.

Since the network of circles establishes repetition, below, the main focus is on variations and we distinguish four instances. These are: (1) the variation of the dominating polygonal figure; (2) the variation of the spatial relations between the circles; (3) the variation of the sizes of the circles; and (4) the variation in the material application.

5.1.3 Variations on a Repetition I: The Hexagon

The most distinctive formal feature in the Seljuk patterns is the polygonal geometry. Equilateral polygons and corresponding stars are frequently used. In line with the cultural context briefly given above, the theological symbolism provides dominant formal features, such as the star motif for the design from the beginning. The guilds guide the style and set restrictions on how much a designer could deviate from the norm. On top of all this, the formal and technical aspects of the creative task introduce more physical constraints. The stone craftsmen work with simple tools – a compass, a straightedge, a chisel. Numeracy is not involved. Thinking in terms of these means and looking at end results, it is assumed that craftsmen initiate their patterns on guidelines drawn or carved lightly onto the material. For practical purposes – and to easily deal with bumpy surfaces or broken edges– these guidelines are drawn with the compass and accordingly were circles. In the examples where the repeated rule is *vesica piscis*, the width of the intersecting area is exactly one radius. Once the compass is at work again, with the radius at constant value, successive steps result in a uniform grid. Each intersection point becomes the center of a new circle. In the successive steps, the designer places the compass needles on the two points of choice. As the second circle is drawn intersecting with the first, new reference points emerge in addition to the center points. This way the craftsmen can actually accommodate small mistakes that might accumulate in their infinitely recurring pattern on irregular surfaces. All the constraints provide a context for cognitive and creative thought processes during the design.

120   *Looking to the Future*

Commonly, the featured polygon is a hexagon. The equal-sided hexagon pops up often once the equilateral triangle grid is superimposed on the circle grid. The designer most definitely knows and anticipates this symmetric and dominant polygon at the earlier stage of drawing the circle grid. However, alternative polygons exist in other designs based on the same geometry. This means that despite the repetitive quality of the underlying system, the design vocabulary is not entirely predetermined. How and why the designer transforms the uniform layout into a distorted motif is surprising. Even if the style of the guild is imposing a structure, the designer acts on what he sees during the design construction. The variety of patterns relies on such actions. These actions could be learnt actions. In other words, the designer may already have these as part of a vocabulary. This does not undermine their importance, however. These are visual jumps that change the course of a design, whether they are premeditated or not. At the same time, some of the parts in the second alternative are kept the same as in the first alternative. Despite the acknowledgment of new intersections that can yield all kinds of adventurous new lines, the designer repeats the hexagonal symmetries. In the end, the visual effect is just a little different while most parts repeat the relations in the first alternative. Third, there is a basis of a relation between the two alternatives. Whereas each alternative seems to be an arbitrary choice when viewed in isolation, their similar origins and features (parts) associate them with one another. We can appreciate this association only because we are observing it both in the process and in comparison. This is the fundamental pedagogical tool in these pattern constructions.

It is that the designer sees rather than the image that is seen from the point of view presented. Valid alternatives are abundant, albeit dependent on purpose and context, these examples are valuable as illustrations of visual thinking at work. The dynamics are similar to those of ill-defined design problems where the problem definition keeps changing during the design activity.

5.1.4 Variations on a Repetition II: The Underlying Circles

As mentioned above, when the designer starts on the blank surface, the first step is drawing circles with the compass. Once the designer puts down the first circle, there is a new formal reference system to build on. The perimeter and the center point of the circle provide references to relate to. In the following stages, as more circles are added, what the designer sees (prefers to see) may keep changing, and in turn create new references. If the designer repeats the same rule, a consistent group of relations emerge.

The size of the first circle determines more or less the scale of the entire project in relation to the surface. Similarly, its location determines how the overall composition will be positioned. There is a good chance that they are related to the overall design in the craftsman's head: how the patterns will fit the edges of the surface or how the pattern is visible from a certain distance. It may well be that the possibilities considered by the designer are limited, based on his cognitive capacities, on cultural restrictions, or on contextual preferences. Nevertheless, it is useful to understand these choices as a part of a much larger set of infinitely many choices in order to appreciate the relations that are in fact implied in these choices. For example, vesica piscis is an instance in a series where the distance between the centers of two circles gradually increases. If we look at the spatial relationship of vesica piscis, two properties are easy to pick out: the radii of the two circles are equal, and each of the centers is on the circumference of the other circle. If the second property is omitted, one can have indefinitely many spatial relations with two identical circles. What directs the choice of the designer is the parametric relation to the larger whole, which in this case can be the type of polygons anticipated in the next step or the final design. This helps in evaluation as well. And if the choice is to be reconsidered, alternatives are known. If we keep increasing the distance between the centers but the radii of the two circles are not equal and have a ratio of 1:2 instead, a new series of possible relations emerges.

All this speculation is assuming that the craftsman would be technically able to do this as well. With a compass of two chalks at the end of a rope, he can just fold the rope in half for the half measure. Some of these spatial relations with the half-size circles can guide him in dividing his initial circle, expanding or contracting it. The half measure is easy to guess and easier for the craftsman to do. But he could also shorten the rope to arbitrary lengths by rolling it around the chalk or his finger. In

122 *Looking to the Future*

many Seljuk patterns circles of different sizes result in motifs that combine varying sizes of stars (Bakirer, 1992). It is possible to explore many other series where the ratio of the circle radii is changing. All series are similar in principle. Most of their elements are equal in definition in terms of circumference and center relations. There are an infinite number of these series for all the different ratios of radii.

For the uniform circle grid that was described at the beginning of this section, the iterative application of a simple rule is sufficient. Nonetheless, if the designer leaves the constraint of using the intersection points as center for new circles, new results can be achieved.

The designer's choices are in general very particular. He sets and follows rules repetitively but there are new reference points to consider each time rules are applied. In existing examples, there are more than a couple of ways to create polygonal infinity pattern guidelines with circles. Intertwined circles, depending on how they are connected, give different angled grids at the intersection points. Executed examples are commonly based on a triangular/hexagonal grid, but rectangular/octagonal ones are also frequent. Whereas the hexagonal comes out so naturally in a process with the compass, the octagonal one is possible as long as the designer is using a parallel ruler. Some of the most stunning examples are pentagonal. One could do much more with the same two circles. The design space is infinite.

5.1.5 *Variations on a Repetition III: Size of Parts*

The underlying system of repeating circles sustains properties such as axial and rotational symmetry, closed or incomplete polygons, and lines that extend over the surface. These are repeated features that help us identify the style and are dependent on the circle grid. Deviations in pattern designs mostly start when straight lines are superimposed on top of the circles. The design space is infinitely rich during the design process and the designer's path is deemed finite and unique only after the fact.

During the design, once a circle grid is created, one can also invent fields of different densities. The designer may see new points of reference for himself at the intersections of circles and straight lines. New circles of a different size may emerge from this set. Instead of lines then, one could be drawing circles to connect the intersection points. Similar to the possibilities at the very beginning of the design when the canvas was still blank, new circle grids can be acquired. In the same circle grid, an alternate grid of larger circles is constructed and areas with larger hexagons emerge.

There are indefinitely many descriptions of a developing shape like this. There are just as many descriptions for connecting the lines in the intersection point grid. Recognizing new parts in a shape is possible only if the world is viewed in part relations rather than distinct and pre-set object properties and classifications. The designer's deliberate actions determine the choices along the way and the final results. The alternatives to a designer's path may not be legitimate without a real context, but the process is ideally open to just about anything.

5.1.6 *Variations on a Repetition IV: The Weave*

Once the shape is finalized and the craftsman starts using his chisel to carve, a new level of materiality is introduced. The craftsman calibrates how thick he wants his shapes to be according to the brittleness of the stone and the space in between the shapes. He then proceeds to carve out the centers. The braiding comes later as a "face treatment." Nevertheless, just as much as the earlier process that takes the design from intersection points to hexagon, the weaving effect suggests that the craftsman's view is holistic. The weave pattern repeats in most examples. There is a reason: the designer establishes which end of the line he starts hitting with the chisel or what sequence he follows. In the overall composition, the order of which line gets chiseled out first is important. Variations in that order would result in hexagons that interlock differently.

In other motifs, we see that the designer is sometimes able to depict infinite rays rather than enclosed shapes, despite the hexagonal or octagonal geometry of the overall design. This is especially impressive and confusing if the final motif alludes to polygons but the lines acting as design elements do not follow a predictable weave pattern. The design can consist of rays that shoot off the edges of the frame instead of interlocking polygons.

124 *Looking to the Future*

5.1.7 Seeing the Broader Picture

There are endless possibilities for each of the four variation themes above. There are also many more themes one can explore. The design strength of the Seljuk patterns comes from the abundant potential to explore a versatile structural canvas, namely, the interlocking circles. There are other examples in design, some already shown in this book, to argue for the value of rhythm as a relation of repetition and variation. At a first glance, geometric patterns may seem to involve less creativity in comparison to the more complex formal exercises in architectural design. However, these patterns have the essential minimum to talk about visual richness and the variety in perceiving parts. The restrictions of the trade make it easier to pinpoint that minimum. The visual jumps that change the developmental course of a pattern design are moments of selection in an infinite space of possibilities. These selections are not predictable to those outside the trade. Still, with the right balance of repetition and variety, meaningful designs are possible.

Meaning in both cognitive and creative processes is the associations one makes with precepts, through recognized features – regularities– in specific contexts. Richards, Feldman and Jepson (1992) propose the idea that key features in objects and events play an essential role in acquiring meaning in perceptions. The argument follows that in the attempt to construct meaning in an object, preference is usually given to the most familiar/associated feature in that context. This is all framed by the regularities one has so far acquired. Preferences, and thus regularities are context-specific. They are formed as part of our upbringing, and pertain to a particular world. People with different upbringings, thus different contexts, have different preference orders for features. The design process is rarely the conversion to a key feature that is pre-set. Rather it is the diversion from it. This holds true for variations among the repetitive features of Seljuk patterns as well. Designers rely on repetitions to diverge from in pursuit of novelty.

In general, a designer's process shows that one specific individual's perceptive context can vary from time to time. This is crucial in a creative process. One must acknowledge that a key feature is only a transiently ideal condition, even for one individual. The properties can be reinterpreted and new ideals can be devised to address different intentions. The

Computational Design Foundations   125

key feature is the result of the Gestalt perceived at that present time. This is possibly why the craftsman is not following the grid *per se*. His decisions are based on other key features than those assumed by us, outsiders, or even what he initially thought they were. The social, material, historical contexts all impose on perception. Discoveries are made in the canvas as the eye switches from one coordinate frame to another. Differences to be discovered among repeating features are just as much a positive challenge to the designer as they are to the viewer.

The ways in which this book looks at the designer's process leaves out a lot of the trivial conditions. Here the designer or the craftsman must have hundreds of different seeing instances of an irregular stone surface, with his chisel tapping in the wrong direction once in a while, or tapping a tad too much into some of the shapes. Also, he is probably more spontaneous than in the limited illustrations of the process shown here. If we were to look at the original design, most of the shapes are not exact. There is even more room for variation through the imperfections. The geometry that the craftsman uses gives way to indefinitely many perceptions and designs. There are hundreds of similar designs that are known. All this spontaneous action operates on changing key features and preferences.

Seljuk patterns are full of repetitions, mainly because of the craft limited by the technical and cultural traditions. However, within all the limits, there are points of freedom, especially if we accept the production of these patterns as a visual process where the designer takes the initiative. Hence, all part relations cannot be defined beforehand. They will arrive at the scene just as the designer does, but they cannot be predicted. It is not only inefficient but simply inhibiting to foresee that definitively. If I am to define absolute features for a circle, which polygons will I be missing out on in later steps? Circles are the beginning guidelines only and they set a consistent ground to walk on and break away from where necessary.

Choosing options is an incomplete description for design which is really a decision process in an act of creation. A designer assumes that their choices are close to being unlimited each time there is a decision to be made. The choices are unlimited despite a rationale that is deliberate and particular to the designer and to the circumstances. The designer, at

126   *Looking to the Future*

any point, can change their reasoning to another consistent path of thought. The visual step-by-step computation of the patterns, as assumed in this chapter, undermines presumptions that will inhibit the process at any stage. It is essential that these patterns are visually constructed and not blindly copied entirely based on a previously configured model. Visually informed decisions can reflect the unique path of the designer's pre-ferences just as shown for Ross and Dow previously. This too offers a lesson for modern-day – design– computing at a foundational level. For the purposes of basic design, approaching these patterns as computa-tion is significant because the relation of that unique path to the broader design space is better appreciated when formal relations between design elements are analysed comparatively. In addition to better understanding the working methods of the past, a computational approach to geometric constructions of patterns has the potential to turn into a design learning methodology as it may be used to understand and convey basics of design.

5.2 Talking, Formally, about Basic Design: Visual Schemas

Getting the design students to talk about designing is just as important as getting them to design. Otherwise, the final products, that lack criteria, are the only means to evaluate the education received. If, however, the students vocalize to themselves as much as to others, the questions and the possible answers they have regarding their thinking and designing processes, they might improve and increase their learning. This is a way to vocalize the *reflection-in-action* and is even more significant in a foundations studio where the reflection habits are being established for the first time for the purposes of designing.

Previous chapters have shown that the view that design is to be talked about, explicitly, is not a new one. As early as the turn of the nineteenth century, Denman Ross introduced the issue of *how to* in the forefront of *what to* in design education (Özkar, 2005a). Fortunately, more and more educators now acknowledge the growing role of process over the pro-duct in technologically integrated design processes. Despite heated debates, the interest and the conviction in explicit design processes accelerated with the Design Methods movement (Broadbent, 1979) and continued with the notion of diagrams (Do and Gross, 2001). More and more integrated with information technologies, the contemporary paradigm of architectural design calls for open and dynamic processes of design. Today, more design ideas and processes are depicted through various, perhaps unclear but nevertheless seductive and stimulating diagrams, and this is encouraging for the growing field of inquiry into design methodologies and techniques.

Similarly, in more design studios, methods that enable actions and critical discussions regarding the product are coming to the forefront. There is a good amount and breadth of literature regarding the various technical, social, pedagogical, and practical issues surrounding the state of the art in design education, some with a focus on the studio. To mention a few key references, Findeli (2001) provides a comprehensive discussion of multiple aspects of the general topic, while Oxman (2008) gives an accurate and extensive account of the impact of digital technologies on design education, and Stiny (2006) introduces a computable connection between *doing* and *talking* in design. Looking from the point of integrating computer technologies into design curricula as enablers of contemporary design processes, the studio, particularly the foundations studio, seems to be the place where one not only to learns to produce but also learns to talk about design. The purpose of talking in the foundations studio is twofold: first, understanding and developing design skills, all the while connecting them with the general notions of computation, in order to liberate thinking/reasoning from the association with quantitative and hierarchic structures alone, second, as part of a holistic view of design and design education where the student (the novice designer) is at the center as the actor of learning.

Beginner architecture students often display their discouragement when discussing what is, to them, internal, unclear, and sometimes accidental in the work they produce. They often come with preconceptions of how designers behave, based on the common market imagery of the architect and/or architecture lacking social and rational foundations. Encouraging students to talk about what they do is a significant step in demystifying the notion of design in their eyes. Talking changes the image of the designer into an accessible one and shows that design is to be criticized based on various valid criteria, is learnt and developed. The

128   *Looking to the Future*

first year in architecture education is where the culture and habits of design thinking start to form and where the students are introduced to its tools for the first time. As tools of representation and thinking are constantly revised with the changing technology, it is necessary that, for the sustainability of a contemporary design education, students acquire early on an awareness of the dynamic nature of design knowledge.

There is a growing literature on the student/learner-centered higher education paradigm, which is relevant to any scholar engaged in curricular or course design. Brown (2003) recapitulates the necessary conditions for it and the psychological factors involved. Although well beyond the scope of this book, some of these factors and conditions, such as active and hands-on learning, students' motivation, and social development, are in line with what is epitomized here in talking. Talking in the studio involves asking questions, playing different roles, comparing, seeing, and doing something just to try it out as actions of self-reflection in a process of production. The studio environment is often considered the ideal setting for a learner-centered higher education paradigm, but every studio setting does not by default fit this model. The key is in sustaining the attitudes and the discussion environment for the student to self-reflect and develop their own position in action. Where enabling the student as an active and self-critical subject is a key matter of concern, basing studio learning on dialogue (through questions, panel discussions, critiques, etc.) is a common starting point. Nevertheless, more than just words, formalisms are needed for this conversation to be linked with the visual and spatial thought processes and eventually computation.

5.2.1 Means to Talk, Formally, about Basic Design

In foundations studios in architecture schools across the world, tasks are often deemed abstract and removed from real design problems similar to the early educational models a century ago. First and foremost, the learning outcome is the design thinking experience and accordingly, the ability to relate various forms at different levels of complexity. Defining relations (some arrangement of what is conceived as separate parts) is usually a more complex task when there are fewer constraints in how to perceive the parts and wholes visually, as there are multiple levels and alternatives in perception.

Talking in the studio does not have to be formal, but formalisms are handy to follow, repeat, and help to document the talking. The basic premise here is that basic design exercises are visual/spatial computations (Özkar, 2005b). Ideally, showing that their design works as a visual computation helps the student to observe what they are doing, to accommodate it within one's own mind and to develop it further. Basic design exercises seem especially suitable to be observed within shape computation formalism as they deal with less complex forms and relations. However, as basic design exercises display their own level of complexity due to their abstract nature, conveying the formalism of visual rules to the beginning student proves not to be as straightforward. This book aims to draw attention to the practicality of the matter by showing what kinds of formalisms are relevant to the students' discussions in the context of basic design.

Shape grammars have been presented and widely used as devices of talking about design. Many scholars have worked towards integrating the formalism of shape grammars to design education. In various levels of architecture education, the formalism has been valuable in helping the students to recognize and develop further the systemic, recursive aspects of their design, as well as the generative aspects of rule-based systems and parametric assemblies towards contemporary production processes. Knight (2000) has been one of the key promoters in architecture and has diligently been encouraging architecture students to bring their design processes to terms with visual rules. While Celani (2002) emphasizes recursion in design in her valuable attempts at introducing the shape grammar formalism to her students early on, Sass (2005) incorporates rule-based processes with fabrication. Additionally, there is a wide variety of tools that have been developed to provide an interface to the shape grammars formalisms (Chase, 2005).

The general idea of integrating the shape grammar formalism in the foundations studio is to incorporate shape rules as well as the knowledge of visual algebras and Boolean operations into the vocabulary of studio talk, in support of the conventional panel discussions. Hypothetically, similar to pointing at the visual composition with a finger and

130 *Looking to the Future*

elaborating a visual relation with words, using rules should be an efficient and shared way to talk about design decisions. However, a few attempts quickly show that for any basic design there are too many visual relations to consider for shape rules. The abundance is confusing and futile unless one also talks of some higher-level relations between the shape rules. The proposal is that visual schemas, generalized versions of rules (Stiny 2006, 2009b), come in handy when talking about the higher-level relations. In the studio environment, the number of rules to be discussed increase and the meticulous representation of each and every one of them loses any practicality. The argument based on these cases is that when different students operate within one schema, it is good to compare rule variations and learn from them. There are too many visual rules and no grammar that can be finally set, whereas schemas are general devices that help compare, group, categorize, associate, contextualize, and vary rules. Students do not discuss every single possible rule but have the chance to observe, discuss and learn that rules of the same schema are good for doing different things.

Visual schemas are more general ways to understand design decisions, processes, methods, whereas a visual rule can have more specifications. Schemas are represented in abstract ways such as x→y but still refer to shapes. Ross's insistence on triangles as a grid, and Dow's horizontal and vertical frame divisions are also schemas. The difference is that they are not represented in a format with an arrow in between the before and after as in the computational approach. As will be shown in the two examples below, similar design processes can be represented with visual schemas and visual rules in the context of basic design. Visual schemas provide a more suitable level of discussion than the detailed shape rule formalism for the foundations studio talks.

5.2.2 Founding Design Knowledge: Recurrence, Emergence and Visual Schemas

In the keynote speech he gave to the 2009 meeting of the ECAADE, Stiny (2009b) emphasized once again the indispensable connection between recursion and embedding in the context of design computing. In addition to the usual coupling of recursion with the identity relation in symbolic computation, Stiny proposes that in design computation, part relations,

Computational Design Foundations 131

specifically embedding, are indispensable partners to recursion. Recursion and embedding constitute a significant part of design knowledge in the context of computation and have played their parts, in the form of rule-based systems and emergence, in numerous practices of visual computation in design. Stiny's emphasis was a reminder of the simultaneity of the two aspects. This book suggests that these two notions are among the foundational design knowledge to be primarily conveyed in basic design exercises and that visual schemas are suitable for doing so.

Recursive functions in design computing have been acknowledged before (Stiny and Gips, 1972; Stiny, 1985; Kirsch and Kirsch, 1986). Existing examples of shape grammar applications in education have mostly explored the recursive aspects of design via additive approaches, starting out with initial shapes set in some spatial relation which are iterated in space as relevant addition rules of the type $x \rightarrow x+t(x)$ are applied. Basic design exercises, as abstract compositions, are not unlike these processes. They inevitably rely on recursion, or rhythm, to use a designer's term, as it establishes links between the parts, of similarity or variance, which in turn help the eye in reading what makes up the unity in a composition.

It is useful to identify the two common ways, one additive, another subtractive, of setting up basic design problems. An example to the additive approach would be something along the lines of "organize the given shapes in space" and an example of the subtractive approach would be something along the lines of "carve shapes out of a solid material." If the aim of a unified whole is also given, both approaches are usually treated as composition. However, they differ greatly in the level of plasticity they provide. Compositions with primitives mostly tend to be orthographic (easily measured, geometrized, and cut) and carving seems to promote free hand movements.

Both types of basic design problems encourage embedding and recursion but the emphases are different. One can argue that while additive processes run the risk of limiting one to discrete parts and pre-set structures, subtractive processes may encourage part embedding. The ice-ray examples (Stiny, 1977) are comparable to the second type. Parameterized divisions provide flexibility in changing how the rule is applied similar to

132 *Looking to the Future*

the subtractive approach. Rules are applied in changing ways. Working with an interpretable whole provides more creative operations than working with conceptually constrained initial shapes (Özkar, 2004). Dividing the whole into consequent parts uses recursion as much as an additive process. But since each recurrence deals with what is emergently left over from, or has been previously an embedded part of the step before it (rather than a composed new whole, as in addition), these subtractive processes might be further explored as a way to convey to the students the emergence of new wholes alongside of recursion.

Oxman (2002) describes emergence as visual cognition and distinguishes between the syntactic and semantic structures involved. The advantage of shape grammars over the symbolic rule-based approaches has been the open door for emergence, enabled by seeing. Semantics are left to the subject and syntax to circumstance. Emergence of new shapes in additive shape computations allowed for dynamic and creative generative processes with indeterminable results and large design spaces. Moreover, the embedding part relation allows for the emergence of new parts all the time.

The two examples in Section 5.2.3 will follow the thread of additive schemas and emerging shapes. One of them starts with a given additive schema and the other starts with an already designed whole, asking what possible schemas might have been used. While inquiring into how formal ways to talk about design can be introduced to first year architecture students, this book suggests expanding on these notions with visual evidence from these two basic design examples.

In line with Stiny's conceptualization, a design schema is also described as a visual form of generic design knowledge (Oxman, 2000). In the context of design education, Oxman and Streich (2001) propose that the acquisition of the ability to represent design knowledge and the basic visual schema are part of learning in design. To the best of the author's knowledge, visual schemas have not been particularly discussed with reference to foundational design exercises. With emphasis on the cognitive aspects of what they imply, a computer model has been developed to support the representation of visual schemas and cognitive processes in design (Oxman, 2000). Additionally, with the

Computational Design Foundations 133

purpose of providing a formal description to design exploration with sketches, Prats et al. (2009) show how schemas correspond to design rules in a process and use visual schemas to correlate different designers' visual rules.

First and foremost, schemas are rule types. Stiny (2009a) specifies some of these as $x \rightarrow \Sigma t(x)$, $x \rightarrow x+t(x)$, $x \rightarrow x$, $x \rightarrow x'$, $x \rightarrow x+x'$. The first is a recursive prescription that can be classified under the very first schema given above. A visual rule that complies with this schema and describes the problem well is Rule in Figure 5.2. One square is replaced with nine, each some Euclidean transformation of the first.

The verbal expression, which can also be imagined as a description of a design task in the studio, is "take a square composition, and create nine Euclidean transformations of it, then arrange these nine transformed square compositions in a three-by-three larger square." In this visual schema, one looks for and works with changing form relations between the various parts of each square composition as they side with the parts of another square composition. New parts and wholes as well as other visual schemas constantly emerge. The task turns out to be more than the additive one prescribed in the beginning. Here, one is encouraged to see, within the bounds of a given set of confining rules, and to explore multiple variations. In the end, the sum of the units yields new wholes (more than the sum of parts) because their parts can be configured into new shapes (Figure 5.2).

As the task is not necessarily a one-step computation, one can also choose to use this other schema $x \rightarrow x+t(x)$ to start putting units together two at a time. Many rules fit this schema, one of which is "add one square to any one side of the original square." It is possible to conceive an alternate spatial relation/rule where the two adjacent units have line parts that align rather than meet perpendicularly.

The second example illustrates two variations. Comparison is a powerful tool in design teaching. Viewing two works produced for the same task side by side provides an opportunity to talk about how to read design rules similar to the silent game (Habraken and Gross, 1987). In reading a fellow student's design work, one identifies visually recursive patterns, relations, and visual schemas. We look at two compositions in Figure 5.3. Let us assume a general schema that transforms the first composition

134 *Looking to the Future*

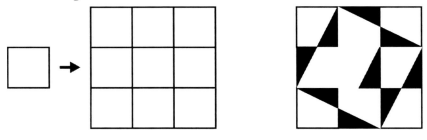

Figure 5.2 A visual rule and its application in design.

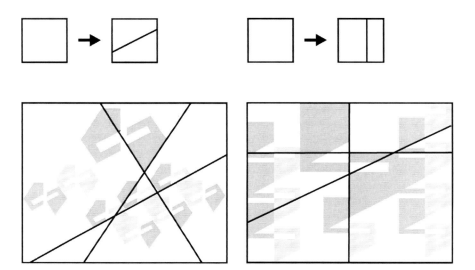

Figure 5.3 Two visual rules and their application in similar designs.

into the second one: x → x'. This example was originally of two compositions produced by two different students where the second one improved on the work of the first. Here, that narrative is omitted and the compositions have been improved by the author for the purposes of focusing on the relations. Shapes change a little; some parts and relations are carried on. The number of shape groups increases in the second work. However, one big group is more or less centrally located in both. The schema for both the first and the second work individually is x → t(x).

Another schema recognized in the first work is the schema to organize the page. Parts are arranged in alignments and this could be specified in two rules in Figure 5.3. The first rule is employed by itself in the first composition whereas the second student creates a second rule which is a variation of the first rule in the same schema and uses both. This is similar to the visual rules discussed in the context of other basic design problems (Ozkar, 2005b) and the visual guides that Ross draws repeatedly on the photographs. The two rules in Figure 5.3 are similar to those produced in earlier chapters for Dow. It is promising that not only schemas but sometimes rules as general as these are recurrent in various design problems. The two rules are especially significant to showcase the slight variations within a schema and what different outcomes it can result in. Here, the second work applies the schema in the first with a slight variation for the overall design in how it fits an orthogonal page frame.

As a result of this variation, the axes for shape alignments differ from the first to the second. The second application of the schema takes into consideration the orthogonal frame of the canvas along with the angles of the parts.

5.2.3 Generic Schemas

Formalisms are not a direct way of talking about design in the foundations studio where seeing and doing are emphasized. Formal ways to talk about design actions are conventionally encouraged and so far they have mostly been drawings, or the products themselves in addition to words that are transferred from daily life. A novice designer's vocabulary is slowly developing through discussions. It is a worthwhile idea to include shape grammars to these formal ways but shape grammars and proper visual rules are external devices that are difficult to incorporate into the already heavy intellectual and physical load. Students are not going to be bothered with abstractions (the notion of computing with shape rules might as well be abstract to them) in an environment where they are constantly being encouraged to think visually and spatially, and the number of potential rules is quite high. Pointing at some relation while trying to come up with a good descriptive word, or at best a

136 *Looking to the Future*

concept, is the practice. Nevertheless, rules can be talked of as simple as two shapes connected with an arrow, and to compare and contrast these, visual schemas seem to be relevant. Rather than a seamless mathematics of shapes that do not add up to a sensible grammar, the schema is easier to grasp, and it addresses, with benefits, the need for formalism.

The schemas discussed in relation to the two examples here also signify the design knowledge conveyable in the foundations studios. First, emergence is not only the occurrence of a new shape in a linear generative process, but also a recognition of a shape that was there before but not seen. This is generally what is referred to as the ambiguity in shapes, but can be extended to emergence if one understands it with reference to the changing context. In the examples discussed, shapes are parts of wholes and co-existing parts act in the emergence of new shapes despite the fact that these shapes are already there to begin with. Hence, there is a need to talk about emergence as ambiguity in a general sense. More generic schemas can be devised in future studies, for example, to include $b(x)$ or $prt(x)$, as it is mostly boundaries or parts that the eye sees in a different light.

Similarly, recursion in design is more complex than a linear iteration. In basic design exercises, repetition or rhythm, emerges as an organizing schema and is rarely linear. It develops in multiple dimensions and multiple instances of it co-exist. In architecture education, repetition, not only as an additive approach, but also in decomposing wholes into parts, emerges as a strong schema for making sensible and unified wholes.

Recursion and emergence culminate in variation, which includes not only repetition but also similarity and change all at once. A schema of variation could be that rule A $(x \rightarrow x + t(x))$ varies into rule B $(prt(x) \rightarrow x + t(prt(x)))$. Variation is a strong tool to teach design and is easily talked about with visual rules/schemas. For example, the schema $x \rightarrow x + y$ (or the visual schemas above) might help in comparing and contrasting rules where y is varied with one constraint and understanding/ recognizing/discussing organizational decisions. Visual rules help not only in generating alternative solutions but also in creating controlled variations of one solution as a way of testing and making mistakes and retracing. Being able to vary (according to a theme if needed) is an important skill to acquire for a beginning design student.

In short, schemas help identify, generalize, and convey the key aspects of relational and reflective thinking: recursion, seeing emergent shapes, as well as parts, boundaries, and relations, and building up variation, prior to learning proper shape rules and design grammars.

These are initial ideas to locate formalism in the studio. More inquiries are required to systematically develop and test ways. Interdisciplinary collaborations may be useful in addressing pedagogical, cognitive and instrumental aspects of the problem in a unified manner. Moreover, there are many more rule types to be explored in conjunction with basic design exercises. Any hierarchic relation to be explored between the types may also be helpful for students.

These analyses set up examples to better understand design computations with visual schemas. They show that visual computations co-exist at multiple levels in the visual design processes, and that parts and wholes are interrelated and different wholes are causally related. Both examples show that different simultaneous perceptions of parts exist. Complexity is due to the parallel processing of shapes. Schemas are a way for the beginner students to understand this complexity and how to work within it. Moreover, visual computations are not literally just limited to the visual. They are coupled with labels (for example, information relevant to the application of the rule), such as assumptions about a certain part (for example, the Gestalt notion of continuity) and material properties (for example, properties that are assigned weights). Schemas encompass all these traits and set up a good prequel to learning about more explicit shape computations in more advanced-level design studios.

Note

1 This chapter consists of excerpts from relevant work previously published elsewhere and, with permissions from the publishers, revised for this book for the purposes of connecting the content of the first four chapters to more recent investigations. Section 5.1 is excerpts from my chapter in an edited volume. See Özkar, M., "Repeating Circles, Changing Stars: Learning from the Medieval Art of Computation," in N. Lee (ed.) *Digital Da Vinci: Computers in the Arts and Sciences* (Berlin: Springer, 2014), pp. 49–64. Section 5.2 is excerpts from my article published in *Nexus Network Journal* in 2011. See Özkar, M., "Visual Schemas: Pragmatics of Design Learning in Foundations Studios," *Nexus Network Journal*, 02/2011, 113–130.

138 *Looking to the Future*

Bibliography

Bakirer, Ö. *Selçuklu Öncesi ve Selçuklu Dönemi Anadolu Mimarisinde Tugla Kullanimi* [The Use of Brick in Anatolian Architecture in Pre-Seljuk and Seljuk Era]. Ankara: ODTÜ, 1981.

Bakirer, Ö. "Aksaray Cincikli Mescid'in On Yuzundeki Geometrik Orgu Duzenlemelerinin Tasarimi Icin Bir Deneme," IX. Vakif Haftasi Kitabi: Turk Vakif Medeniyetinde Hz. Mevlana ve Mevlevihanelerin Yeri ve Vakif Eserlerinde Yer Alan Turk-Islam Sanatlari Seminerleri, 2–4 Aralik 1991 Ankara (Vakiflar Genel Mudurlugu Yayinlari, Ankara, Turkey), 1992.

Bakirer, Ö. "Story of the Three Graffiti," *Muqarnas*, v. 1 (1999): 42–69.

Broadbent, Geoffrey. "The Development of Design Methods." *Design Methods And Theories*, v. 13, n. 1 (1979): 25–38.

Brown, David. "Learner-Centered Conditions That Ensure Students' Success in Learning." *Education*, v. 124, n. 1: (2003): 99–104, 107.

Celani, Gabriela. "CAD – The Creative Side – An Educational Experiment That Aims at Changing Students' Attitude in the Use of Computer-Aided Design." 6th Iberoamerican Congress of Digital Graphics.Sigradi, 1: 218–221, 2002.

Chase, Scott C. "Generative Design Tools for Novice Designers: Issues for Selection." *Automation in Construction*, v. 14, n. 6 (2005): 689–698.

Do, Ellen Yi-Luen and Mark Gross. "Thinking with Diagrams in Architectural Design." *Artificial Intelligence Review*, v. 15, n. 1–2 (2001): 135–149.

Findeli, Alain. "Rethinking Design Education For The 21st Century: Theoretical, Methodological, and Ethical Discussion." *Design Issues*, v.17, n. 1 (2001): 5–17.

Habraken, H. John and Mark Gross. *Concept Design Games (Books 1 and 2)*. Cambridge, MA: Design Methodology Program, 1987.

Kirsch, J. L. and R. A. Kirsch. "The Structure of Paintings: Formal Grammar and Design." *Environment and Planning B*, v. 13 (1986): 163–176.

Knight, Terry. "Shape Grammars in Education and Practice: History and Prospects." *International Journal of Design Computing*, v. 2 (2000). Available at: www.mit.edu/%7Etknight/IJDC/. 2000.

Lawson, Bryan. *Language of Space*. Oxford: Architectural Press, 2001.

Lefebvre, H. *Rhythmanalysis: Space, Time, and Everyday Life* .Trans. S. Elden and G. Moore. New York: Continuum, 2004.

Mülayim, Selcuk. *Anadolu Turk Mimarisinde Geometrik Suslemeler*. Ankara: Kultur ve Turizm Bakanligi Yayinlari, 1982.

Ogel, Semra. *Anadolu Selcuklularinin Tas Tezyinati*. Ankara: TTK, 1966.

Oxman, Rivka. "Design Media for the Cognitive Designer." *Automation in Construction*, v. 9, n. 4 (2000): 337–346.

Oxman, Rivka. "The Thinking Eye: Visual Re-Cognition in Design Emergence." *Design Studies*, v. 23, n. 2 (2002): 135–164.

Oxman, Rivka. "Digital Architecture as Challenge for Pedagogy: Theory, Knowledge, Models and Medium." *Design Studies*, v. 29, n. 2 (2008): 99–120.

Oxman, Rivka and Bernd Streich. "Digital Media and Design Didactics in Visual Cognition. Architectural Information Management." 19th ECAADE Conference Proceedings. Ed. H. Pentilla, Helsinki, Finland, 2001: 186–191.

Ozdural, A. "Mathematics and Arts: Connections between Theory and Practice in the Medieval Islamic World." *Historia Mathematica*, v. 27, 2000: 171–201.

Özkar, Mine, "Cognitive Analyses and Creative Operations." In John Gero, Barbara Tversky, and Terry Knight (eds), *Visual and Spatial Reasoning in Design III*, Key Center for Design Computing and Cognition, Sydney: University of Sydney, (2004), pp. 219–229.

Özkar, Mine. "Form Relations in Analyses by Denman Waldo Ross: an Early Modernist Approach in Architectural Education." Aesthetics and Architectural Composition, Proceedings of the Dresden International Symposium of Architecture 2004. Ralf Weber and Matthias Amann (eds.), Mammendorf: pro Literatur Verlag, D-82291, 2005a, pp. 322–328.

Özkar, Mine. "Lesson 1 in Design Computing Does Not Have to Be with Computers: Basic Design Exercises, Exercises in Visual Computing." In José Pinto Duarte, Gonçalo Ducla-Soares, and Zita Sampaio (eds) *Education and Research in Computer-aided Architectural Design in Europe (eCAADe) 23 Digital Design: The Quest for New Paradigms*. Lisbon: eCAADe and IST, 2005b. 311–318.

Özkar, M. "Visual Schemas: Pragmatics of Design Learning in Foundations Studios." *Nexus Network Journal*, v. 02 (2011): 113–130.

Özkar, M. "Repeating Circles, Changing Stars: Learning from the Medieval Art of Computation." In N. Lee (ed.), *Digital Da Vinci: Computers in the Arts and Sciences*. Berlin: Springer, 2014, pp. 49–64.

Özkar, M. and Lefford, N. "Modal Relationships as Stylistic Features: Examples from Seljuk and Celtic Patterns." *JASIST* v. 57, n. 11, (2006): 1551–1560.

Prats, Miquel, Sungwoo Lim, Iestyn Jowers, Steve W. Garner and Scott Chase. "Transforming Shape in Design: Observations from Studies of Sketching." *Design Studies*, v. 30, n. 5 (2009): 503–520.

Rasmussen, S. E. *Experiencing Architecture*. Cambridge, MA: The MIT Press, 1959.

Richards, W., Feldman, J. and Jepson, A. "From Features to Perceptual Categories." In D. Hogg and R. Boyle (eds) *British Machine Vision Conference 1992*. New York: Springer, 1992.

Sass, Larry. "A Wood Frame Grammar: A Generative System for Digital Fabrication." *International Journal of Architectural Computing*, v. 4, n. 1 (2005): 51–67.

Shlokovsky, B. "Art as Device." Trans. Benjamin Sher. In *The Theory of Prose*. Bloomington, IN: Dalkey Archive Press, 1991 [1925].

140 *Looking to the Future*

Stiny, George. "Ice-Ray: A Note on the Generation of Chinese Lattice Designs." *Environment and Planning B*, v. 4, n. 1 (1977): 89–98.

Stiny, George. "Computing with Form and Meaning in Architecture." *Journal of Architectural Education*, v. 39, n. 1 (1985): 7–19.

Stiny, George. *Shape*. Cambridge, MA: The MIT Press, 2006.

Stiny, George. "Recursion, Identity, Embedding." Course lecture at SIGGRAPH. 2009a.

Stiny, George. Keynote lecture at eCAADe, 2009b.

Stiny, George, and Gips, James. *Shape Grammars and the Generative Specification, Best Computer Papers of 1971*. Ed. O. R. Petrocelli (ed.) Amsterdam: North Holland, 1972, pp. 125–135.

6 Conclusion
Pragmatics of a Foundational Studio

It is often thought that students who apply to study in design schools should have certain skills and abilities to draw or sketch freehand. Motivation and a perceptive eye are really all that is needed. Perceptiveness is not merely a cognitive trait, but also the attitude and skill that come from an understanding that definitions of things might change. Throughout a training in design, biases in methods, techniques, and materials will constantly be altered as individuals master them in their own ways, discovering new things to do with them along the way. Conventions are required in education towards a professional degree just as much as in communication. However, biases and conventions are not absolutely necessary to begin with. Basic design education, which is practiced today as an introductory and formative course in architectural education, is based on starting from a clean slate, free of professional terminology and focusing on fundamental and abstract terms. The main incentive behind it is to equip the student with a core set of design knowledge, elementary skills of dexterity, and a fortified sense of accountability to others. At the end of a course, the student is expected to have implicitly or explicitly understood that creative thinking is both a personal process and reasoning that feeds on surprising interactions with materials, situations, and other dynamic actors. These are key to the beginning of a design education.

In an age of rapid developing design and production technologies, it is now more important than ever to endorse design as fundamentally a reasoning process. The more romantic view of design excludes reasoning from the creative process. Assuming that reasoning is deterministic holds

142 *Looking to the Future*

design back in the use of new tools. Design is reasoning that uses visual and tactile resources to creatively react to constraints. Interaction with intellectual and technical tools is an active part of design. I have proposed in this book that Ross and Dow's work, in contrast to the rigid approaches of the early twentieth century, is a case in point.

Creativity is possible in a reasoning process where definitions vary. To be able to talk of creative processes in design, designers do not have to compromise either the reasoning or the uncertainties of experience that are crucial to their process. The creative process is not static and does not have a set vocabulary. It is continuous. In order to maintain it as such, it is important to convey to novice design students that the creative process is a thought process that explores uncertainties and redefines constraints.

The basic design curricula in many schools today try to encourage students to see creativity from a pragmatist viewpoint. Two features of the basic design studio are key in realizing these explorations as similarly seen in the methods of Ross and Dow. First, the content matter is abstract forms and abstract problems. The simplicity of these forms helps students focus on form relations, but also serves another purpose. Unfamiliarity of abstract forms brings variance in perception. This triggers thinking, and taking action to understand, make up or develop definitions. As a result, the student is expected to make new sense out of form relations and undertakes the responsibility to do so. This is often what makes the first year studio difficult to psychologically deal with. Second, basic design builds upon the ideas of repetition, comparison, and variance. The student is encouraged to develop unique ways to deal with the material and problems at hand, all the while acquiring a conscious governance over the process and the choices made along the way. Exercises demonstrate that definitions change as the students interact constantly with the material in the process, and that students are able to assess these interactions comparatively over time. There are no predetermined value systems, but only contextual handling of materials and problems. Visual and tactile involvement is encouraged, rather than verbal, to surpass habitual thinking. Repetition endorses the recognition of similarities and variance.

The basic design course set-up is a studio that provides grounds for experimentation and exploration of possibilities. How to reach design through this open experimentation is left to the student without any pre-defined formula. In the end, each student acquires a unique individual understanding of it. Yet, the important task is to convey to the student that their process is to be understood, represented, and shared as reasoning. The common oversight is to revert to defining timeless basic elements and aesthetic values. But reasoning does not necessarily depend on a finite, universal vocabulary. Rather, it develops with definitions that continuously are changing. This idea, illustrated in Ross and Dow's pedagogical approaches, is the potential in the basic design studio set-up. Showing similarities with Ross and Dow's devices of abstraction, visual rules and schemas are powerful tools to expose the students to the experience of tracking and controlling the process. The primary focus should be to convey to the students that visual rules and schemas are flexible. The dynamic use of rules certainly is the core of basic design education and should be perceptible throughout. This would also be the early integration of a computational perspective to design education.

Basic design, as a pedagogical term, entails much less ambitious concepts than the fundamentals of composition. "Basics" refer to isolating the design problem in the relations between material and other external qualities. Abstract forms that are the signature of basic design education are tools to isolate and focus on form relations. Form is not the objective of a basic design problem. Rather, the aim is to consciously produce it. This is the compelling aspect of approaches presented in the first two chapters of this book. Arthur W. Dow unassumingly draws attention to a simple formal relation and its varieties instead of trying to teach the rich complexity of a landscape. It is no doubt important for a painting instructor to talk about and stir an awareness in the student of the full sensory experience and everything else that could be said about the landscape. However, it is just as important to provide the basic tools to suggest how to act in that experience. Dow's abstraction demonstrates some of the compositional relations in the landscape drawing. This puts emphasis on form relations in learning design, rather than presumed forms of experience.

These underlying relations that Dow chooses to establish support the pedagogical motivations behind basic design to show that the designer

144 *Looking to the Future*

establishes the relations between form and things. Basic design deals with simpler forms to draw the focus on giving a fundamental understanding of how the designer establishes form relations. These simpler forms should not be interpreted as fundamental relations or forms that universally apply. They are arbitrary and contextual. For example, however common they are, the triangle, square and circle, which Kandinsky introduces as primary forms, are arbitrary shapes. Different from Best Maugard, Kandinsky, Moholy-Nagy, and Neurath, Dow and Ross refrain from defining a basic formal vocabulary. First, they focus on form relations rather than forms. And assessed with reference to organizational concepts such as harmony, balance, and rhythm, these relations are as vague as they can be. Second, the form relation that is singled out in Dow's example, the perpendicular lines, as well as those in Ross's analyses, the triangles, are singular and quite simplistic. They may not be special for anybody else nor in another context. Dow acknowledges its commonality, and teaches it so, as simply a principle of design. Different from a formalist approach, Dow uses it to show how to abstract. Ross's remarks in a lecture he gave at Rhode Island School of Design on the object of design education are testament to his position along the same lines: "teaching not merely what to do but how to do it" (1903, 10–11).

The pedagogical value of abstract forms and form relations is twofold. One is the simplifying aspect that helps the student initially focus on a small number of form relations. It allows for contemplation on how relations are established, or can change. For this purpose, Arthur W. Dow explores variations that share only a few constraints: a set number of perpendicular lines and the square frame. The rules that Dow applies in these variations are not easily decipherable. Although there are common elements in most of Dow's compositions to give clues to his sensibilities, Dow does not specify the reasoning behind each variation. However, based on what is common to the variations, the general visual rule can be as shown in the far left of the top row (Figure 6.1). This is a dividing rule that says draw a perpendicular line inside the square to divide it into two unequal areas. How Dow applies this general rule in each variation is Dow's visual preference. A similar example by basic design instructor Maurice de Sausmarez, years later, explores "a variety of area divisions of a square" (1964, 38). In the text that accompanies these and ten more

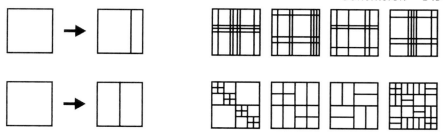

Figure 6.1 Two visual rules and their applications in similar designs.

different divisions of a square, de Sausmarez does not specify the reasoning behind each. However, his rule is simple enough to decipher. De Sausmarez uses just one rule of division (vertical line through midspace of square) and he is able to apply it in various ways to explore "a seemingly infinite number of possibilities" with just that (ibid., 38). This rule is shown in the bottom left of Figure 6.1. This is the simple form relation that makes all the other variations possible. The ways in which this is visually applied bring about the variation. The perpendicular line is not simply added, but done so rather selectively. Why these selections are made is not so much the point of this example, but that they are possible. De Sausmarez writes that the system could be "on a basis of mathematical proportion or intuitive" (ibid., 38). The mathematical proportion is exemplified in the division across the mid point. The intuitive, or the utility of senses, is exemplified in Dow's division of the square. De Sausmarez's schema is really an instance of Dow's general rule and the other illustrations in Figure 6.1 all show variations based on these two slightly different rules.

In a student's design process, a spatial relation may look just right and this would be a rule. But the student would be expected to be able to identify it. The next time the rule is applied, the student might see it fail and discard it. Even arbitrary rules are rules. The student would benefit from seeing what is going on, and rules facilitate that. De Sausmarez's variations for the squares, together with Dow's, offer a simple model of a visual reasoning process in design. The reasoning is characterized in the rule and its applications. A perpendicular line that divides the square into two equal areas is the only spatial relation and the rule that gives the directive to do so is the only rule in this example. All variations repeat

146 *Looking to the Future*

the same rule, multiple times, in different combinations. De Sausmarez focuses on one spatial relation, because even then, there are indefinitely many possibilities. Basic design assignments usually give abstract forms and/or specify frameworks. In most exercises, students are asked to arrange abstract forms without altering the general framework while exploring the variety in application of a few rules. In de Sausmarez's example, there was only one rule. With reference to this rule, we are able to talk about its various applications where squares are picked out from an accumulation of lines.

The Dow and de Sausmarez rules simply show how the system of abstraction leads to new designs that follow similar principles. To refrain from relying on what one knows about the world, the inquiry could be furthered in exercises where the relationships are questioned and new rules are tried. Unfamiliarity, the other pedagogical aspect that is introduced by abstract forms provides the basis for this. Abstract forms detach the thought process from habits. Their unfamiliarity helps the student understand and experiment with changing definitions. For example, Ross's wallpaper patterns keeps the focus of the design problem in relations rather than in forms, by keeping the shapes not simple but unfamiliar. Units in Ross's wallpaper patterns are significant from a basic design point of view because of their unfamiliar forms. The student visually thinks how these forms might relate to one another. Variety emerges in the process. It is possible that shapes in those patterns had a different degree of familiarity to the students a hundred years ago. But Ross is aware of the value of abstract forms, when he chooses these exercises as a part of his curriculum. Exercises similar to Ross's wallpaper patterns are often practiced in basic design studios today. Irregular abstract forms allow the student to consider first how to recognize features in these forms and then how their features might come together.

From edible items to amorphous everyday objects, anything can be treated as an abstract part for a basic design exercise. The central theme to the exercise would be thinking about how these forms can correlate. Designers are continually interested in exploring and creating new relations between things. There is value in working with unusual material in that new form or part relations are by default discoverable. The thought process involved is mostly constrained by how the shapes are perceived.

As preferences are made momentarily in the interaction with the materials and tools, the students understand and develop personal reasoning in a given context to identify features of shapes and use those features. More importantly, however, the students must be able to show how they position these forms together, whether the arrangement was a one-step process or involved multiple thoughts. The aim is for the students to develop a way of questioning each step and to be able to project from it towards some other process.

As iterated above, simple forms and contexts aid in training the individual to strategize based on what is at hand and at that moment. Basic design in an educational context is not intended as a prototype for professional design. It is not even a laboratory where simplified versions of realistic problems are tested out. Abstract forms rather offer unfamiliar contexts for thought experiments that focus on form relations. Basic design is prior to any architectural knowledge and deliberately neglects this knowledge to benefit a creative process. In an abstract design problem, meanings, or definitions, are temporarily projected based on what is perceived then and there. Design rules are different, or differently applied, every time. Diagrams, popular thinking tools in design practices, employ the same idea. Most contemporary architects obscure the contexts of the design problem in abstract diagrams in order to strategize with new set of constraints that emerge from these.

Following the arguments above, no value systems should be imposed on the student in an educational environment. The sole value that basic design can offer to support is the accountability, the obligation the student develops towards fellow humans in holding oneself responsible for the consequences of design decisions. Often in basic design studios, assignments end in general discussion together with the students. For example, a discussion starter could be to ask the students to start grouping the student work according to criteria that they come up with, or to ask whether any student work has successfully applied an idea. This is not as judgemental as discussing successful projects right away and pointing out what is a good work. The discussion may never converge to a point. It serves the purpose, however, if by the end, students are exposed to multiple readings as well as their own and start to make judgements on their own.

148 *Looking to the Future*

Variance changing definitions and all the uncertainties that designers cherish are common practices in the basic design curricula since basic design aims at the personal development of the student. But for this to be a self-conscious development, the experimentation that results in design needs to be understood as a reasoning process. This is usually not obvious enough. The lack of a fixed structure for thought does not correspond by default to the lack of reasoning. Pedagogically, simple forms are tools to develop basic relations between concepts. A relational view of the world contradicts general orders that classify things according to predetermined conceptions. It rather offers changeable characterizations to what may be a part and what may be perceived as a whole. In addition to comprehending given constraints through investigations with the material and apparatus, one develops personal constraints to lead one's own design process. Reasoning is contextual and does not conform to universal generalizations. It needs to be more obvious as such in basic design exercises as well.

Basic design education usually demonstrates that there are a variety of rules and that the students can develop their own. This is primarily because each student apprehends that he or she is doing things differently from the others. Personal rules also keep changing. But all this variation often gets overshadowed by general discussion, a general framework that tends to be loaded with concepts such as balance, and harmony, or the stylization of the minimalist geometry in use. The interaction with other students in the studio tends to converge different ways into one. In that case, the studio turns into a determined exploration of one ideal. All this sharing and interaction is not necessarily bad, but each student needs to understand that they must develop their own rules. Contexts, rules, and goals are all dynamic. The constraints given in each problem need to change accordingly. The set-up must guide the student not towards a preferable design product but to a self-conscious process.

The kind of problems that are given, as well as how the end discussions are executed, is important. Tentativeness and seemingly vague tasks are popular. But questioning, and while doing that, understanding how to strategize, are imperative. There is value in recording the process. Figure 6.1 shows that even if it is one rule that is recorded, it holds

Conclusion 149

the key to many variations that are comparable. Rather than being overwhelmed with possibilities, the advantage is the student is encouraged to understand how he or she develops ways to reason.

As demonstrated in the abstract means to talk about the basic design exercise in Chapter 5, rules can be used to represent the actions taken during a design process. However, there is no direct way to convey that process is representable through rules to the student who will not have a developed sense of what a rule is in its flexible definition. One primarily needs to grasp the changing aspects of a design process to understand a concept of dynamic rules. Allowing for personal narrations, visual rather than verbal, is one idea suggested in the previous section. Rules are already implicitly recorded in design processes through models and drawings. Slowing down the process will only demonstrate how the individual sets up constraints and reasons through continuous perceptual shifts. Figure 6.2 illustrates a perceptual shift. Two initial shapes, a triangle and a square are given and are to be placed on a shared symmetry axis. The figure on the left shows the spatial relation. Then a rule is introduced to erase the triangle. There are two choices to apply this rule. One application takes away the smaller triangle, and the other takes away the large one. The two figures on the right shows the two possibilities side by side. The variation here exemplifies sagacious thinking. The formalism for such representations is given in George Stiny's computational theory (2006).

The representation of the process with discrete rules should not mislead the student or professor into thinking that the design process has fixed discrete parts or steps. Rather, the purpose of the rules is to make the conceptual changes explicit. Discrete parts of a design process are helpful, however, in communication with others especially in computational methods.

Figure 6.2 Two triangles out of one.

150 *Looking to the Future*

The primary motivation for this book has been to develop a context of ideas to discuss creative thinking as a relational reasoning process. Although this motivation emerges in and for a contemporary setting, and with computational design in mind, the primary interest for writing the book was to create a missing background. Looking at the origins of relation between computational thinking and basic design in nineteenth-century thought introduces a refreshed context to both. It also revives the Pragmatist discussion on senses as a link between the two for a reconsideration of the terms reasoning and senses together today. Certainly, hundred-year-old perspectives are obsolete in many ways. However, the end of the nineteenth century stands as a unique period between the conservative past and the present in terms of how the mind–body problem is perceived. Thus, this interpretation sets a frame for understanding alternative origins of the idea of computation in design. The book was never intended to give full historical accounts of the people, movements and theories mentioned. The theoretical inquiry would benefit from including broader assessments with contemporary perspectives in philosophy and cognitive science as well as technological developments that bring about new modes of designing. Further studies would also touch on the problems existing today with the interaction of architecture and other research disciplines, such as computer science. Moreover, a continuing study may result in the designs of a complete curriculum for a beginner studio.

A secondary motivation for this book has been to re-emphasize the importance of basic design education from a refreshed point of view. The nineteenth-century context of ideas included educational reforms that put emphasis on active learning, student psychology, and hands-on experimentation and these ideas found parallels in the works of Denman Ross and Arthur Dow. Their work, and the background they emerged from, paved the way for the twentieth-century developments in education and the basic design instruction, as it came to be understood today. Looking back at the nineteenth-century origins as well as the medieval geometric construction of patterns brings a perspective that reconsiders the utility of visual and tactile senses in design education. As the production technologies and the maker culture are fast spreading, design reconnects with the arts and crafts in new ways yet again.

The book did not elaborate on the concept of learning separately from the broader term of education. William James claims sagacity and learning are the two indispensable parts of reasoning. He writes:

> The art of the reasoner will consist of two stages:
>   First, sagacity, or the ability to discover what part, [M], lies embedded in the whole S which is before him: Second, learning, or the ability to recall promptly M's consequences, concomitants, or implications.
>
> (James 1983, 957)

Throughout the book, the narration followed the ability to see emerging shapes. Focusing on reasoning as a whole, it accentuated the use of sagacity in making the most of uncertainties. Learning, on the other hand, requires further reflection and possibly a separate discussion. In the sense that James refers to it, learning is by habit, and is part of a different philosophical, or rather physiological, discussion than that of learning in design education. In its place, the reference is to Stiny's changing rules. Habitual learning in reasoning can be described using consistently recurring rules, but it dilutes the general discussion of this book. The argument, from a creative point of view, has been to call attention not to how people hold on to what they know, but rather that they can discard it. The book addressed the question of learning, in a more general sense: learning, in the case of basic design education, is the student's awareness and competence in changing rules in personal design processes.

Finally, in an attempt to emphasize the importance of basic design education in the technological context today, this book presents basic design as a precursor to integrating computation to design education. This stems from the observation that basic design material allows us to think about what designing is at a fundamental level with ever-changing rules that the designer creates and/or manipulates. Especially now in an age of emerging technologies, with the intention of preparing the student not only to design but thinking about design as computation, basic design studios can incorporate the concept of rules more rigorously. Computation can be reflective of the design process. In this way creative thinking is not compromised in design and in computation. At this

152 *Looking to the Future*

point, it is important to note that there is also a pedagogical aspect to computation. How do we teach design thinking? How does a student learn to appreciate the qualities of a designed object? What to learn in design? The geometric construction of patterns, and traces of similar guidelines that Ross and Dow separately used to manipulate form relations towards achieving unity, composition, coherent wholes, and good designs, all provide thoughtful precursors to a core of design education that is full of recurrence, shape emergence, and visual rules and schemas that are directives for design action. Design as such is interlinked with computation. In a basic design education, such pedagogical computing can aid the competences expected for the student. In learning by doing, technical skills in dealing with materials, mastering tools and communicating ideas as well as spatial and analytical thinking abilities can be grouped as some of the skills to be gained. Students also gain knowledge of the organizational principles that are summarized here as repetition and variation as well as of the materials and methods that they use. Last but not the least, as the computational approach in utilizing visual rules and schemas for design enables the student to share and be accountable while establishing a context for design decisions, students also learn social and ethical positions as attitudes. These outline what foundational design knowledge to influence the later years of architectural education might be today when considered as pedagogical computation. Defining the design process as reasoning with uncertainties and sagacity is important to set models to those who create tools of abstraction for designers. Designers should compute in the way they design. Showing visual rules as an integral representation of design will not immediately change how computers work. But with the growing research interest in it, visual, and now material, computing devices are the makings to integrate computation into design education early on. At the least, they would reinstate the designers' confidence in how they reason.

Bibliography

De Sausmarez, Maurice. *Basic Design: The Dynamics of Visual Form*. New York: Reinhold Publishing Corporation, 1964.

Dow, Arthur Wesley. *Composition: A Series of Exercises in Art Structure for the Use of Students and Teachers*. Berkeley, CA: University of California Press, 1997 [1899, 1920].

Conclusion   153

James, William. *Principles of Psychology*. Cambridge, MA: Harvard University Press, 1983.

Ross, Denman W. Address on Design: Public Exercises at the Dedication of the Memorial Hall. Given at Rhode Island School of Design. Tuesday, November 24, 1903. Biographical and general information relating to Denman Waldo Ross, ca. 1880–ca. 1935. HUG 1753.400. Harvard University Archives.

Stiny, George. *Shape: Talking about Seeing and Doing*. Cambridge, MA: The MIT Press, 2006.

Index

A Theory of Pure Design 11–2, 17–8, 20, 25, 29, 31, 42, 84
absolute 61, 81
abstract: form 2–44, 47, 64, 84, 88–96, 142–7; form relations 25, 38, 47, 69, 90, 96, 144; shape 15, 93
accident of vision 63, 74
Alexander, Christopher 86, 93
American Arts and Crafts 4, 11, 35
American Pragmatism 47, 48, 51, 83
analytical modes of design thinking 7
Arnheim, Rudolf 58, 97, 101
art and design education 4, 11, 46
Asia Minor 117
attitude: as competence in higher education 45 111, 128, 141, 152; to design 101

Bakirer, Ömür 112, 118, 122
balance: to balance 39, 56; with harmony and rhythm 12, 17–18, 30, 36, 86, 88, 144, 148
basic relations 37, 148
basic vocabulary 93, 97, 144
basics of design 2, 88, 92, 118, 126, 143
beauty 12, 13, 24, 29–30, 53–5
Best Maugard, Adolfo 92, 99, 144
blocks: building 15, 45, 97–9; kindergarten 72–3
blurred image 63
bodily experience 5
Boston 3, 83–4,
boundary 16, 41–2, 68

canon 14, 36
Carnap, Rudolf 96–7, 99–100
Celani, Gabriela 129

Classical: paintings 23, 26, 28, 30; architectural education 88
cognitive 119, 121, 124, 132, 137, 141
Columbia University 3, 35, 63, 83, 85
combinatorial 20, 49
communication 2, 96, 141, 149
compass 112, 117, 119–22
competence 45, 111, 151–2
conservative 3, 13, 98–9, 150
continuity: between subject and object 52; visual 117, 137
crafts 12, 14, 45–46, 57, 64, 73, 94
craftsmen 118–9, 121, 123, 125
creative thinking: as computation 151; in education 64; progressive 83; perceptiveness in 90–1, 101; as reasoning process 141, 150; as scientific philosophy 102; self-conscious 2, 86–7

De Sausmarez, Maurice 144–6
decorative arts 16, 47, 64, 83–4
Design as Science 11, 36
design pedagogy 1, 57, 64, 96, 102
design technology 86, 111, 127, 151
design thinking: and material world 46, 60, 94; as discipline 3; as reasoning 5, 7, 12; learning about 114; 128, 152
Dewey, John 63–4, 83, 91, 102
diagram 25–7, 55, 71, 84, 127, 147
dynamic worldview 47, 50–1
dynamics of abstract form 6

embedding 49, 116, 130–2
emergence 130–2, 136
emerging shape 20, 132, 151

Index   155

emerging technologies 86, 151
empathy 58, 60–2, 64, 93, 96
empiricism 47–8, 98
engineering 86
evanescent moment of experience 62, 65

fabrication 1, 7, 129; *see* also Sass, L.
fabrication technology *see* production
   technology
Fenollosa, Ernest 3, 52–3, 55, 74, 84, 90
grammars 129, 132, 135, 137
Frank, Marie 11–3, 22, 40, 90
Froebel, Friedrich 45, 56–7, 71–3, 85, 93–4
Fry, Roger 31, 47, 87, 92
functionalism 92–3, 97, 100–1
functionality 17, 48, 52, 86

Galison, Peter 99–100
geometric patterns 112, 117, 124
Gestalt psychology 12, 60, 96–7, 101
Gestalt switch 50, 58–60, 69, 125
grid *see* guideline; *see also* Klee, Maratta
Gropius, Walter 14, 88, 90, 99, 101
guideline: abstract 6, 38, 40, 50, 71, 73;
   Dow's 43, 71; in background grid 20,
   26; in material application 118–19; in
   uniform grid 25, 128; triangular 20, 22,
   68–9; underlying 21–2, 31

hand: of the subject 30; using of 41, 73,
   131
hands-on learning 5–7, 45–7, 85, 89, 93,
   128, 150
harmony *see* balance
Harvard Psychological Laboratory 94
Harvard University 3, 11, 14, 25, 63,
   83, 94
higher education 2, 4, 128

ice-ray 131
Illustrations of Balance and Rhythm
   6, 11, 15,
Impressionist art 41, 43, 63, 84, 89, 92
individual learner 4
infinity 117–8, 122
initial shape 131–2, 149
intellectual tools 6, 30, 43, 75, 96
intellectualism 4, 51, 85, 101
Ipswich, MA 3, 35, 83, 85
Islamic 112, 117
Itten, Johannes 28, 57, 60–1, 93, 99

James, William 4, 47–52, 60–5, 87, 90, 95,
   98, 151
Japanese influence 40, 53, 84, 89, 92
Jarves, James Jackson 12–3
Jones, Owen 17, 86, 92

Kandinsky, Wassily 56, 97, 99, 144
keen eye 31
Kindergarten 2, 57, 73, 93
Kindergarten Association, PA 35
Klee, Paul 71, 113
Knight, Terry 129

La Farge, John 39, 42, 58, 62–4
Ladovsky, Nikolai 93–6
laws of: perception 94; proximity,
   similarity, closure, good continuation,
   symmetry 96
learner-centered 46, 128
learning by doing 45, 152; *see also*
   hands-on learning

Maratta, Hardesty G. 21–3, 25–6, 72–3,
   112
Martin, Marianne W. 4, 11
material context 1, 64
material properties 137
mathematics 118, 136
Moholy-Nagy, Laszlo 92, 144
Mülayim, Selcuk 118
Münsterberg, H. 4, 90, 94–5
Museum of Fine Arts in Boston 84

natural: forms 17, 53, 55, 88; scenes 28,
   36,
network 71–2; *see also* guideline
Neurath, Otto 97–100, 144
New Bauhaus 101
Nonrepresentational form 13
Norton, Charles Eliot 12, 83
notan 40–1, 43, 55, 59
Nute, Kevin 52–3

O'Keefe, Georgia 11
Ogel, Semra 118
On Drawing and Painting 11
optimization 86, 111
order 12–3, 25, 30, 48, 55, 58, 73, 87,
   113–4
organic: form 53, 84; system 53–5; unity
   51–3

156 *Index*

organicism 47, 51–4, 56, 88
organizational: means 18, 20, 114, 144; purpose 21; relations 27; structure 42, 121, 136, 152
Orientalist 4, 84
ornament 14, 17, 64, 83, 86, 92, 117–8
orthogonal guide 20, 23, 27, 66, 72, 87, 135; see also guideline
Ozdural, Alpay 118

parametric design 7, 39, 121, 128
Parker, Edgar O. 50
part-whole relations 6, 19, 46–7, 56–7, 98, 115, 136
parts see part-whole relations
perceptiveness 47, 57, 86–7, 90–1, 101, 141
personal development 6, 43, 46, 57, 148
Pestalozzi, Johann H. 45, 85, 93; see also Froebel
picture-writing 36, 61
plurality 51, 65, 86
Pointillism 42, 63, 89
Pollock, Jackson 115
polygonal 119
Pope, Arthur 11, 87
Post-impressionists 89
production technology 141, 150

reciprocal 23, 25, 66, 68
recurrence 130, 132, 152
reference point 68, 119, 122
Rhode Island School of Design 46
rhythm see balance
Ruskin, John 11–12, 83

sagacity 6, 47, 49–50, 65, 69, 73, 85, 151–2
Saranlı, Türel 45
Sass, Larry 129
science 13–4, 36–7, 64–5
Second World War 62, 97, 101
Seljuk 112–3, 117–26

Senkevitch, Anatole 94–6
sensory experience 4, 6, 46, 83–4, 93–5, 143
shape emergence 152
Singerman, Howard 12, 46
Stankiewicz, Mary Ann 11, 17, 46, 74–5, 87
star of David 25, 60
STEM 2
Stiny, George 49, 73, 116–7, 127, 130–3
student-centered see learner-centered
symmetry 15–6, 53, 71, 84, 88–9, 91, 120
system of triangles 68

tactile 73, 85, 142, 150
Teachers College; see Columbia University
thematic composition 13
triangulation see guideline

uncertainty 61–2, 64–5, 71, 86, 98–9, 101, 142, 148, 152
unity 31, 52, 87, 99, 117, 131, 152
University of Chicago 101

van Eck, Caroline 52
vesica piscis 25, 117, 119, 121
Vienna Circle 96–7, 99, 101
visual: abstraction 36–7; computation 7, 129, 131, 137; education 96–98; perception 62, 85, 95, 98; rule 50, 69, 75, 100, 129–30, 133–6, 143–5, 152; schemas 126, 130–3, 136–7
VKhUTEMAS 7, 93–7
Vorkurs 93

wallpaper pattern 14–31, 38, 49–50, 56, 64, 146

x→y 131–6